REVISE EDEXCEL GCSE (9–1)
Mathematics
Foundation

PRACTICE PAPERS Plus⁺

Authors: Jean Linsky and Navtej Marwaha and Harry Smith

Contents

Using this book

This book has been created to help you prepare for your exam by familiarising yourself with the approach of the papers and the exam-style questions. Unlike the exam, however, each question has targeted hints, guidance and support in the margin to help you understand how to tackle them.

All questions also have fully worked solutions shown in the back of the book for you to refer to. In addition, some questions have videos explaining the working step-by-step. Look out for the QR codes in green boxes. To watch these videos, scan the QR codes with your mobile phone or tablet using a QR reader.

You may want to work through the papers at your own pace, to re-inforce your knowledge of the topics and practise the skills you have gained throughout your course. Alternatively, you might want to practise completing a paper as if in an exam. If you do this, bear these points in mind:

- Use black ink or ball-point pen.
- Answer all questions.
- Answer the questions in the spaces provided – there may be more space than you need.
- In a real exam, **you must show all your working out.**
- For each paper, check whether you can use a calculator or not. This is stated at the start of each paper. You **cannot** use a calculator for Paper 1.
- If your calculator does not have a π button, take the value of π to be 3.142 unless the question instructs otherwise.
- Diagrams are **not** accurately drawn, unless otherwise indicated in the question.
- The total number of marks available for each paper is 80 marks.
- You have 1 hour 30 minutes to complete each paper.
- The marks for each question are shown in brackets. Use this as a guide as to how much time to spend on each question.

Paper 1: Non-calculator
Time allowed: 1 hour 30 minutes

1 Work out -3×-9

$$-3 \times -9 = 27$$

27

(Total for Question 1 is 1 mark)

NUMBER

Revision Guide
Page 2

Hint

$- \times - = +$
$- \times + = -$
$+ \times - = -$

---

2 (a) Work out $9 + 6 \div 2$

12

(1)

(b) Work out $(15 + 5) \times (5 - 3)$

40

(1)

(Total for Question 2 is 2 marks)

Revision Guide
Page 16

LEARN IT!

Use **BIDMAS** to remember the correct order of operations:

Brackets
Indices
Division ·
Multiplication
Addition
Subtraction

---

3 Work out $24.1 - 1.79$

$$\begin{array}{r} 2\overset{3}{\cancel{4}}.\overset{11}{\cancel{1}}79 \\ 1.79 \\ \hline 22.49 \end{array}$$

22.49

(Total for Question 3 is 1 mark)

Revision Guide
Page 7

Watch out!

This is a **non-calculator** paper. Use a written method for this subtraction.

---

4 Write down the 15th odd number.

1, 3, 5, 7, 9, 11, 13, 15, 17, 19, 21, 23, 25, 27, 27 29

29

(Total for Question 4 is 1 mark)

ALGEBRA

Revision Guide
Pages 34, 52

Hint

The first four odd numbers are 1, 3, 5, 7...

Turn to page 132 for complete worked solutions to the questions on this page.

ALGEBRA

 Revision Guide
Page 25

Hint

Substitute, then calculate. Write down each step, and don't try to do everything mentally in one go.

% RATIO & PROPORTION

 Revision Guide
Pages 1, 55

Problem solved!

Plan your strategy:
- calculate 10% of £240
- work out how many lots of this are needed to make £216
- write down the number of weeks as your answer.

Hint

$10\% = \frac{10}{100} = \frac{1}{10}$. You can find 10% of an amount by dividing by 10

---

5 $T = 3x + 2y$

   $x = 5$
   $y = 4$

Work out the value of T.

$3x + 2y$

$3 \times 5 = 15$ $15 + 8 =$

$2 \times 4 = 8$

$T = \underline{23}$

(Total for Question 5 is 2 marks)

---

6   Alan's wages are £240 each week.

He wants to save some money to buy a television.
The television costs £216.

Alan is going to save 10% of his wages each week.

How many weeks will it take Alan to save enough money to buy the television?

$240 \div 10 = 24$ $24\overline{)216}$

24 $216 \div 24 =$

$24 + 4$ $\frac{24}{9}$

 Scan this QR code for a video of this question being solved!

$\underline{9}$ weeks

(Total for Question 6 is 3 marks)

Turn to page 132 for complete worked solutions to the questions on this page.

7   A rectangle is 4 cm by 8 cm.

8 cm

4 cm

4 cm

8 cm

GEOMETRY & MEASURES

Revision Guide Page 79

Four of the rectangles are used to make a larger rectangle as shown below.

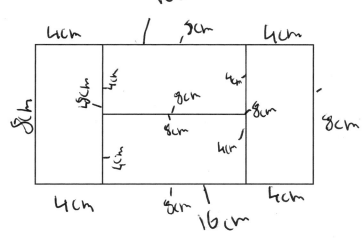

16 cm

4 cm   8 cm   4 cm

8 cm   8 cm   4 cm   4 cm   8 cm   8 cm

8 cm   8 cm

4 cm   8 cm

4 cm   8 cm   4 cm

16 cm

Problem solved!

First label the larger diagram to show the length and width of each small rectangle.

Hint

For part **(a)**, write down the lengths you need to add to get the total perimeter. You can check your working by counting up the number of values you are adding and comparing it to the diagram.

(a) Work out the perimeter of the larger rectangle.

16 + 16 = 32 + 8 = 40 + 8 48

..............................48.... cm
(2)

LEARN IT!

Area of rectangle = length × width

(b) Work out the area of the larger rectangle.

16 × 8

16
 8
‾‾‾‾
128
4

Explore

There are two different strategies for part **(b)**:

1. Work out the length and width of the whole rectangle then calculate the area.

2. Calculate the area of one small rectangle then multiply by 4

Try both strategies and compare your answers. Which did you find easier?

Scan this QR code for a video of this question being solved!

..............................128.... cm²
(3)
(Total for Question 7 is 5 marks)

Turn to page 132 for complete worked solutions to the questions on this page.

3

GEOMETRY & MEASURES

Revision Guide
Page 77

Problem solved!

You could end up in a mess with this question if you don't keep track of your working. Choose a strategy, then write down what you are calculating at each stage.

Hint

Start by working out the total length of the trip, including the stops. Then work out the latest time she needs to start.

Hint

When you have finished, read the last sentence of the question again. Make sure you have given the right piece of information as your answer.

 Explore

Work out the quickest route a delivery driver can use to visit all five towns. Does it make a difference if the driver has to start and finish at the same town?

8   The diagram shows five towns.
It also shows the time it takes to drive between the towns.

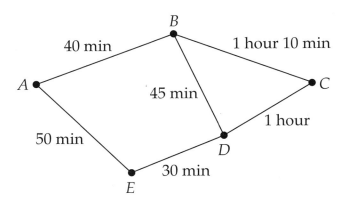

Sue drives a delivery van.

She will start at A, and drive from A to B, then from B to C, then from C to D, then from D to E and from E back to A.

She will stop for 5 minutes in each town to make the delivery. There is no delivery at A.
She wants to be back at A by 4pm.

(a)   What is the latest time Sue can start from A to make the deliveries then drive back to A by 4pm?

$40 + 50 = 90 + 30 = 120 + 60 = 180 + 10 = 250 + 45$

$250 + 45 = 295 + 25$ $60 + 60 = 120 + 60 = 180$

$\begin{array}{r} 80 \\ 10 \\ \hline 150 \end{array}$ $180 + 60 = 240$

$\begin{array}{r} 290 \\ 25 \\ \hline 320 \end{array}$ $60\overline{)320}$ $240 + 60 = 300$

10am.

(4)

Sue decides that she needs to finish her delivery at E by 4 pm and does **not** need to return to A.

(b)   Explain how this would affect the latest time Sue has to leave A.

It would affect because it would take less time to back so she can leave later.

(1)

(Total for Question 8 is 5 marks)

Turn to page 132 for complete worked solutions to the questions on this page.

9

The picture shows a lorry driver standing next to his lorry.
The lorry driver and the lorry are drawn to the same scale.

The lorry driver wants to drive the lorry into a car park.
The entrance to the car park is 3.1 metres high.

Can the lorry driver safely drive the lorry into the car park?
You must clearly show how you got your answer, explaining any
assumptions you have made.

GEOMETRY & MEASURES

Revision Guide
Page 96

Hint

You can use lengths
you know to estimate
other lengths. The lorry
is about twice as tall
as the driver. Write
down an estimate for
the height of the driver,
then multiply by 2

Hint

If you have to use the
height of a person to
make an estimate, you
can choose any height
between 1.5 m and
2 m. Make sure you
write down the height
you are using for your
estimate.

Problem solved!

You have to show how
you got your answer.
That means that you
need to show your
working and explain
what you are calculating
at each stage. Make
sure you finish by
writing a conclusion.

Explore

Practise your
estimating. Estimate
the width and height of
this book in cm, then
check your answer with
a ruler.

Scan this QR
code for a video
of this question
being solved!

(Total for Question 9 is 3 marks)

Turn to page 133 for complete worked solutions to the questions on this page.

% RATIO & PROPORTION

Revision Guide
Pages 13, 60

Hint

Fraction of cards
labelled **X**

$= \dfrac{\text{Number of cards labelled } \mathbf{X}}{\text{Total number of cards}}$

Problem solved!

For part **(b)**, try
different combinations
of cards labelled **X**
and cards labelled
Y in the ratio 2 : 1
Check whether each
combination is possible
given the cards
available, then write a
conclusion.

Explore

If you wanted to
use all of the cards
labelled **Y**, how many
cards labelled **X** would
you need?

10 Here are some cards.
The cards are labelled **X** or **Y**.

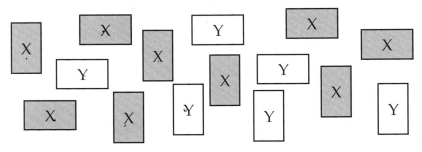

(a) What fraction of these cards are labelled **X**?
Give your fraction in its simplest form.

$x = 9$
$y = 6$ $+ = 15$

$\dfrac{9}{15}$

(2)

Tony takes some of these cards.
He takes cards labelled **X** and cards labelled **Y** in the ratio 2 : 1

(b) Work out the greatest number of cards labelled **Y** he could take.

(2)
(Total for Question 10 is 4 marks)

Turn to page 133 for complete worked solutions to the questions on this page.

11 The table shows some information about the minimum and maximum temperatures in Paris each month from January to May. The temperatures are in °C.

	Jan	Feb	Mar	Apr	May
Minimum temperature	2	3	5	7	10
Maximum temperature	7	8	12	15	19

Show this information in a suitable diagram.

Min
Max

(Total for Question 11 is 4 marks)

Turn to page 133 for complete worked solutions to the questions on this page.

PROBABILITY & STATISTICS

Revision Guide Page 117

Hint

The question doesn't tell you which type of graph to use, so you have to decide for yourself. You need to show **two** pieces of data for each month, so a **dual bar chart** or **time series** would be a good choice here.

Hint

Look at the largest data value before choosing your scale. You need to make sure that the scale on your vertical axis goes up to 20°C.

Hint

Remember to label your axes and include any units. Good axis labels here would be 'Temperature (°C)' and 'Month'.

Watch out!

Always use a **ruler** and a **sharp pencil** to draw any lines or bars.

Revision Guide
Page 56

Watch out!

Don't just guess. You need to show working to explain how you got your answer.

Hint

You need to write both numbers as decimals, or both numbers as fractions before you can compare them.

LEARN IT!

Learn these common fraction to decimal conversions:

$\frac{1}{10} = 0.1$ $\frac{1}{5} = 0.2$

$\frac{1}{4} = 0.25$ $\frac{1}{2} = 0.5$

12 Which is bigger, $\frac{2}{5}$ or 0.6?

Give a reason for your answer.

$$\frac{2}{5} \qquad \frac{6}{10}$$

I converted 0.6 Into

$\frac{6}{10}$ which is bigger

than $\frac{2}{5}$

 Scan this QR code for a video of this question being solved!

(Total for Question 12 is 2 marks)

Turn to page 133 for complete worked solutions to the questions on this page.

13 Here are some coloured cards.

| blue | red | blue | blue | green |

| red | green | blue | green | red |

| yellow | blue | yellow | red |

A card is taken at random.

(a) Which colour of card is **most** likely to be taken?

.... blue
(1)

(b) What is the probability that the card is **red**?

.... $\dfrac{4}{14}$
(2)

James says:

"If there were two more green cards, then green would be the most likely colour of card to be taken."

(c) Is James right?

Give a reason for your answer.

....

....

....
(1)
(Total for Question 13 is 4 marks)

Turn to page 134 for complete worked solutions to the questions on this page.

PROBABILITY & STATISTICS

Revision Guide Page 128

Watch out!

Don't do more work than you need to! Count the number of each colour. You can work out which colour is most likely by finding the most common colour.

LEARN IT!

Probability =

$\dfrac{\text{Number of successful outcomes}}{\text{Total number of possible outcomes}}$

Hint

You don't need to simplify your fractions in probability questions. For part **(b)** write the number of red cards as the numerator of your fraction, and the total number of cards as the denominator.

Explore

Can you describe your answer to part **(b)** in words? Choose one of these options:

| Very unlikely |
| Unlikely |
| Even chance |
| Likely |
| Very likely |

Revision Guide
Page 10

Watch out!

Read the question carefully. It says **estimate** so don't try to calculate the exact amount.

Hint

To work out an estimate round each value to **1 significant figure**.

Problem solved!

For part **(a)** you can keep track of your working by writing words with your answer. You need to find estimates for:

1. The total **cost** of the adult tickets.

2. The **number** of child tickets.

3. The total **cost** of the child tickets.

4. The total cost of **all** the tickets.

---

14 Maninder sold tickets for a concert.
She sold 895 tickets.

597 of these tickets were adult tickets.
The rest were child tickets.

Adult tickets were sold for £19.50 each.
Child tickets were sold for £9.75 each.

(a) Work out an estimate for the amount of money Maninder should receive for the tickets.

$$597 \times 19.50 = 11,641.5$$

$$895 - 597 = 298$$

$$298 \times 9.75 = 2,726.7$$

$$11,641.5 + 276.7$$

£ ....

(3)

(b) Is your answer to part (a) an overestimate or an underestimate? Give a reason for your answer.

(1)

(Total for Question 14 is 4 marks)

Turn to page 134 for complete worked solutions to the questions on this page.

15 Here are some white shapes and some grey shapes.

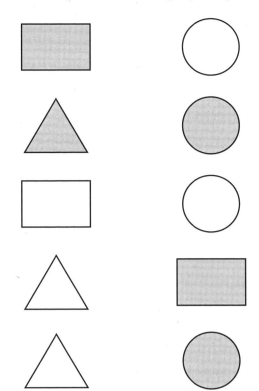

(a) What percentage of the shapes are white shapes?

..................................%

(1)

Ali takes some of the shapes.

$\frac{3}{7}$ of the shapes that are left are white shapes.

(b) How many white shapes and how many grey shapes did Ali take?

White shapes ....

Grey shapes ....

(2)

(Total for Question 15 is 3 marks)

 Revision Guide Pages 13, 55

Hint

Count the number of white shapes and the total number of shapes. If you have to calculate a percentage on your non-calculator paper it will probably be a multiple of 5 or 10. If your calculation looks too complicated, count the shapes again.

Problem solved!

It would be a good idea to check your answer to part **(b)** once you have written it down. Cross off the number of white and grey shapes you have written in the answer space, then work out what fraction of the remaining shapes are white. It should be $\frac{3}{7}$.

Explore

In a packet of sweets, $\frac{3}{7}$ of the sweets are cherry-flavoured. How many sweets could there be in the bag in total? Write down at least three different answers.

Turn to page 134 for complete worked solutions to the questions on this page.

Revision Guide
Page 7

Hint

Estimate the answer before you start. You can use your estimate to check your answer, and to check that you have the right number of decimal places. To estimate, round both numbers to 1 significant figure then multiply:

3.25 → 3 and
0.46 → 0.5 so your estimate will be 3 × 0.5

LEARN IT!

To multiply decimal numbers without a calculator:
- ignore the decimal points and just multiply the numbers
- count the number of decimal places in the calculation
- put this number of decimal places (including zeros) in the answer.

Hint

Work out 325 × 46 then work out how many decimal places to put in your answer.

---

16 Work out 3.25×0.46

2. $3.25 \times 0.46 = 1.495$

....

(Total for Question 16 is 3 marks)

Turn to page 134 for complete worked solutions to the questions on this page.

17 Here is a diagram of a house.

The house is in the shape of a prism.

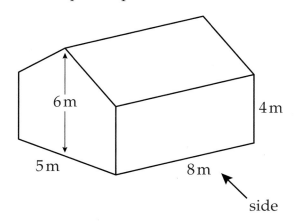

(a) On the grid, draw accurately the side elevation of the house from the direction marked with the arrow.

Use the scale 1 cm to represent 1 m.

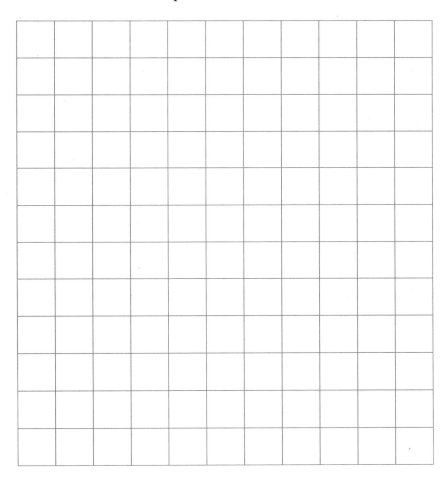

(2)

Hint

When you are drawing plans and elevations you can show a change in depth by adding a line to your diagram.

Hint

Each grid square represents 1 m, so you can count squares to work out the length of each side.

Watch out!

Always use a ruler and a sharp pencil to draw straight lines in your exam.

Turn to page 135 for complete worked solutions to the questions on this page.

Hint

The **plan** is the view directly down from above.

Explore

Here is a sketch of another shape with the same side elevation and plan as the shape given in this question.

Label this shape with any dimensions you can work out. Can you sketch another **different** shape with the same side elevation and plan?

(b) On the grid below, draw accurately the plan of the house.

Use the scale 1 cm to represent 1 m.

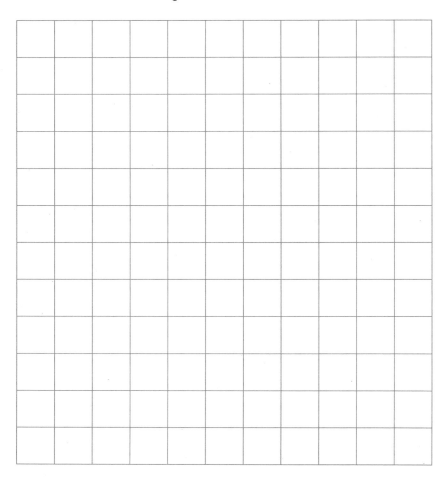

(2)
(Total for Question 17 is 4 marks)

Turn to page 135 for complete worked solutions to the questions on this page.

18 The diagram represents the floor of a village hall.

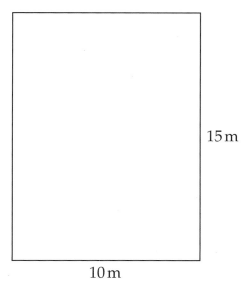

15 m

10 m

The floor is in the shape of a rectangle.
The width is 10 m.
The length is 15 m.

The floor is going to be waxed.

1 litre of wax will cover 20 m² of floor.
The wax is sold in pots of 2 litres.
The cost of a pot of wax is £32.40.

All the wax has to be bought.
Work out the total cost of the pots of wax that have to be bought.
You must show how you got your answer.

£ ....
(Total for Question 18 is 5 marks)

Turn to page 135 for complete worked solutions to the questions on this page.

15

NUMBER

GEOMETRY & MEASURES

Revision Guide
Pages 1, 7, 80

Problem solved!

In a multi-step number problem you should always plan your strategy before you start. Here is a good strategy for this question:

- work out the area of the floor
- work out the number of litres of wax needed
- work out the number of pots of wax needed
- work out the total cost of those pots.

Watch out!

You can only buy a whole number of pots. Look for the smallest whole number of pots you can buy to cover the entire floor.

Hint

Check that your answer makes sense. If it is thousands of pounds, or less than the cost of one pot, then you know you have made a mistake.

RATIO &
PROPORTION

GEOMETRY &
MEASURES

Revision Guide
Pages 64, 98

Hint

Measure the distance on the diagram to the nearest mm, then use the scale to work out the distance in real life.

Watch out!

You might not need to use all of the information in the question. Read part **(b)** carefully and then work out which information you need to use.

LEARN IT!

Write the formula triangle for speed in your working:

$$\text{Speed} = \frac{\text{Distance}}{\text{Time}}$$

---

19 The diagram below is drawn to scale and represents two cities on a map.

Wrexmouth ✕

✕ Lindun

Scale: 1 cm represents 45 miles

(a) Work out the distance, in miles, between Lindun and Wrexmouth.

.... miles

(2)

Robert drove from Lindun to Wrexmouth.
He left Linden at 11 am.
He arrived at 2 pm.

Esther drove from Lindun to Northport.
She drove at the same speed as Robert.
She took 4 hours.

(b) Who travelled the greater distance and by how much?
You must show all your calculations.

(3)
(Total for Question 19 is 5 marks)

Turn to page 135 for complete worked solutions to the questions on this page.

20 Here are the first four terms of a number sequence.

    8   14   20   26

(a) Find an expression, in terms of n, for the nth term of this number sequence.

.................6.................
(2)

Dipen says:

    "124 is a number in this sequence."

(b) Dipen is wrong.
    Explain why.

(2)

The 100th term in this sequence is $5x + 2$

(c) Work out the value of x.

$x = $ ....
(2)

(Total for Question 20 is 6 marks)

$\sqrt{xy^2}$ **ALGEBRA**

 Revision Guide Page 35

Hint

Write the difference between each term of the sequence. Then subtract the common difference from the first term to work out the **zero term**.

LEARN IT!

nth term =
    common difference $\times$
        n + zero term

Problem solved!

For part **(b)** you need to show enough working to explain why 124 is not a term in the sequence. Here are two possible strategies:

1. Write your nth term equal to 124 then solve the equation. If n is not a whole number, then 124 is not a term in the sequence.

2. Write down some consecutive terms in the sequence near 124

Explore

Without showing any working, can you explain why 2017 is definitely not a term in this sequence?

Turn to page 136 for complete worked solutions to the questions on this page.

GEOMETRY &
MEASURES

 Revision Guide
Page 75

Hint

In angle questions like this, the information given in the question is usually **also** shown on the diagram. Parallel lines are marked with arrows, and equal sides are marked with dashes.

LEARN IT!

The interior angles in a quadrilateral add up to 360°

Hint

In an angle problem, always be on the lookout for parallel lines. *BC* and *AE* are parallel, so angle *BCA* and angle *CAE* are alternate angles between parallel lines.

Problem solved!

When you work out a missing angle, write it on the diagram. This will help you with the next step.

21

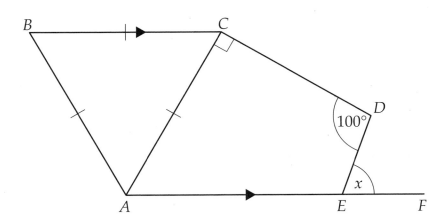

ABC is an equilateral triangle.
AEF is a staight line.

ACDE is a quadrilateral.
Angle *CDE* = 100°
Angle *ACD* is a right angle.

AE is parallel to *BC*.

Work out the size of the angle marked *x*.
Give reasons for each stage of your working.

....

(Total for Question 21 is 4 marks)

Turn to page 136 for complete worked solutions to the questions on this page.

22 Here are three circles A, B and C.

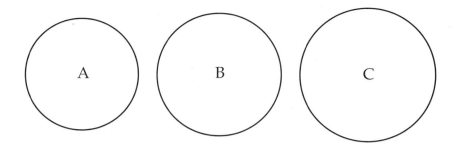

The area of circle A is 200 cm².

The area of circle B is 15% larger than the area of circle A.

The area of circle C is 20% larger than the area of circle B.

Find the difference in area between circle A and circle C.

 RATIO & PROPORTION

 Revision Guide Page 58

Hint

To work out a 15% increase without a calculator:
- divide the original amount by 10 to find 10%
- halve this to find 5%
- add this on to the original amount.

Problem solved!

You need to show all your working neatly to get all the marks. Write down what you are calculating at each stage, and remember to include the units.

Watch out!

Circle C is 15% bigger than **circle B**. You need to work out the area of circle B then increase **that** amount by 20% to find the area of circle C.

Explore

Can you describe the increase from circle A to circle C as a percentage? Would your answer be different if you started with a circle of a different size?

.... cm²

(Total for Question 22 is 3 marks)

Turn to page 136 for complete worked solutions to the questions on this page.

Revision Guide
Pages 37, 42

Hint

Draw a triangle to find the gradient of a graph:

Gradient $= \dfrac{\text{Distance up}}{\text{Distance across}}$

The larger your triangle, the more accurate your calculation will be.

Watch out!

Always use the scale to work out the distance up and the distance across – don't just count grid squares on the graph.

Hint

The gradient tells you how much the cost increases or decreases for each unit of water. You can work out the answer to part **(a)(ii)** by multiplying your gradient by 15

23 Martin's house has a meter to measure the amount of water he uses. Martin pays on Tariff A for the number of water units he uses.

The graph opposite can be used to find out how much he pays.

(a) (i) Find the gradient of this line.

....
(1)

Martin reduces the amount of water he uses by 15 units.

(ii) How much money does he save?

£...............................
(2)

Instead of Tariff A, Martin could pay for his water on Tariff B.

The table shows how much Martin would pay for his water on Tariff B.

Number of water units used	0	20	40	60	80	100
Cost in £	12	18	24	30	36	42

Turn to page 136 for complete worked solutions to the questions on this page.

(b) (i) On the grid below, draw a line for Tariff B.

(ii) Write down the number of water units used when the cost of Tariff A is the same as the cost of Tariff B.

.... units

(3)

Hint

To draw the graph for Tariff B, plot the points from the table and then join them up using a ruler. The point where the graphs cross represents the point where both tariffs cost the same. Read down from this point to the horizontal axis.

Hint

Always read graphs accurate to the nearest small grid square. You need to use a sharp pencil to get accurate readings.

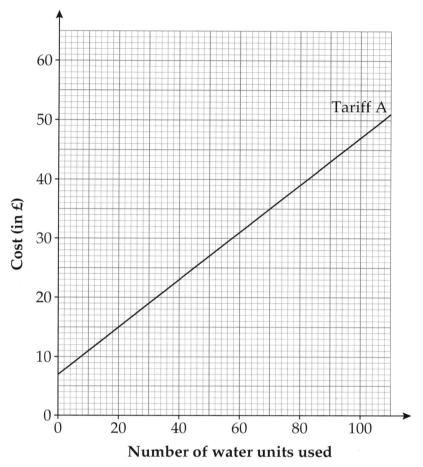

(Total for Question 23 is 6 marks)

TOTAL FOR PAPER IS 80 MARKS

Turn to page 137 for complete worked solutions to the questions on this page.

Revision Guide
Pages 8, 16, 22, 23, 24

Hint

t means 'one lot of t'.

Hint

Write the number first, then write the letters, in alphabetical order, without the × signs between them.

Hint

You can enter this in one go on your calculator.

Hint

Group the m terms and the k terms. Remember the sign (+ or −) goes with the term after it.

LEARN IT!

$a^m \times a^n = a^{m+n}$

Paper 2: Calculator
Time allowed: 1 hour 30 minutes

1 Simplify $3t + 6t - t$

....
(Total for Question 1 is 1 mark)

2 Simplify $e \times 4 \times f$

....
(Total for Question 2 is 1 mark)

3 Find the value of $\sqrt{(1.3)^3 - (0.79 \times 0.3)}$

....
(Total for Question 3 is 1 mark)

4 Simplify $6m + 3k - 2m + 5k$

....
(Total for Question 4 is 2 marks)

5 Simplify $y^4 \times y^3$

....
(Total for Question 5 is 1 mark)

Turn to page 138 for complete worked solutions to the questions on this page.

6   5480 people are at a gig.
Each person has a ticket.
The ticket is coloured red or blue or yellow or green.

2074 people have a red ticket.
1459 people have a blue ticket.
$\frac{1}{3}$ of the rest of the people have a yellow ticket.

Work out how many people have a green ticket.

NUMBER

 Revision Guide
Page 13

Hint

You can find $\frac{1}{3}$ of an amount by dividing by 3

Watch out!

You need to write down your working even if you are using a calculator.

Hint

You can check your final answer by adding up the number of people with each colour of ticket. The answer should be 5480

....

(Total for Question 6 is 3 marks)

Turn to page 138 for complete worked solutions to the questions on this page.

PROBABILITY
& STATISTICS

Revision Guide
Page 128

Hint

Compare the number of segments with the given letter to the total number of segments on the spinner.

LEARN IT!

Explore

How many other ways can you think of to describe an even chance?

---

7   Sally makes a fair 8-sided spinner for a game.

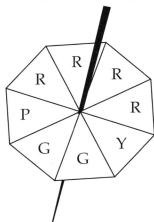

Sally is going to spin the spinner once.
The spinner will land on one of the letters shown in the diagram.

| impossible | unlikely | evens | likely | certain |

From the list above, write down the word that best describes the likelihood:

(a) that the spinner will land on the letter Y

....

(1)

(b) that the spinner will land on the letter R

....

(1)

(c) that the spinner will land on the letter T.

....

(1)
(Total for Question 7 is 3 marks)

24

Turn to page 138 for complete worked solutions to the questions on this page.

8 Express 4 cm as a fraction of 2 m.
Write your fraction in its simplest form.

....
(Total for Question 8 is 2 marks)

Turn to page 138 for complete worked solutions to the questions on this page.

NUMBER

**RATIO &
PROPORTION**

Revision Guide
Pages 13, 61

Watch out!

You can only compare
quantities that are in
the **same units**. Convert
m to cm before you
write your fraction.

Hint

You can simplify a
fraction by dividing
the numerator and
denominator by the
same number.

√xy² **ALGEBRA**

% **RATIO & PROPORTION**

 Revision Guide
Pages 51, 55

Problem solved!

You can use algebra to solve problems like this. Write the amount that Charlotte gets as *x*. Then find expressions for the amounts that Samuel and Ben get. Add all three expressions and set this new expression equal to 69. Solve the equation to find *x*.

Watch out!

Read the question carefully. Ben gives 35% of his share to charity, and you need to work out how much he has left. 100% − 35% = 65% so you can work out 65% of Ben's total to find the answer.

---

9 Charlotte, Samuel and Ben are given some money.

Samuel gets £7 more than Charlotte.
Ben gets twice as much as Samuel.
Together the three get a total of £69

Ben gives 35% of his share to charity.

Work out how much money Ben has left.

£ ....
(Total for Question 9 is 4 marks)

Turn to page 139 for complete worked solutions to the questions on this page.

10 Hafiz is going to cook a chicken.
The weight of the chicken is 2.5 kilograms.

The chicken has to be cooked for 20 minutes for each 500 grams of its weight. He wants the chicken to finish cooking at 1 pm.

At what time should Hafiz start cooking the chicken?

 √xy² ALGEBRA

 GEOMETRY & MEASURES

Revision Guide
Pages 26, 77, 78

LEARN IT!

1 kg = 1000 g, so multiply by 1000 to convert kg to grams.

Watch out!

When you are giving times using the 12-hour clock, you need to write 'am' or 'pm' with your answer.

Problem solved!

Read the information carefully. You can underline important pieces of information. In this question, underline '20 minutes for each 500 grams of its weight'.

Hint

Write the cooking time in hours and minutes. Count back the hours first, then the minutes. Write down the new time at each step of your working.

 Scan this QR code for a video of this question being solved!

....
(3)
(Total for Question 10 is 3 marks)

Turn to page 139 for complete worked solutions to the questions on this page.

PROBABILITY & STATISTICS

Revision Guide
Page 128

Hint

If P(Red) = $\frac{1}{2}$ then exactly half of the segments on the spinner must be red.

Watch out!

The question just asks you to **write** the colours. Don't waste time colouring in your spinner!

Problem solved!

Once you have labelled your spinner, reread the question. **Check** that your answer matches **all** the information given.

---

11 Ayesha is making a fair 8-sided spinner.
The spinner already has the colours red, white and blue written on it.

The probability that the spinner lands on red will be $\frac{1}{2}$

The probability that the spinner lands on blue will be less than the probability that the spinner lands on white.

Complete the spinner by writing on it the colours that are missing.

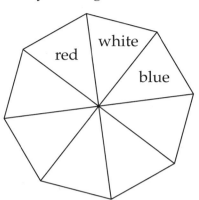

(Total for Question 11 is 2 marks)

Turn to page 139 for complete worked solutions to the questions on this page.

12 Callum wins £300 in a raffle.

He gives 5% of the £300 to charity.

He saves $\frac{2}{5}$ of the £300

He uses the rest of the money to buy clothes.

Work out how much of the money Callum uses to buy clothes.

£ ....
(Total for Question 12 is 3 marks)

 NUMBER

 RATIO & PROPORTION

 Revision Guide Pages 13, 55

Hint

You can use the key to enter a fraction on your calculator.

LEARN IT!

To find a percentage of an amount, divide the percentage by 100, then multiply by the amount.

Problem solved!

You need to **keep track** of your working. Write your working under headings for 'Charity', 'Savings' and 'Clothes'.

Explore

Write your final answer as a percentage of £300. Now convert $\frac{2}{5}$ into a percentage. Can you write down an addition fact involving 100%, 5% and the two percentages you just worked out?

Turn to page 139 for complete worked solutions to the questions on this page.

Revision Guide
Pages 5, 10

There are 60 seconds
in one minute.

Hint

You will need to write a
sentence to state any
assumptions you made.

Watch out!

Make sure you write
down enough working
to justify your answer.

13 A book has puzzles graded easy, medium and hard.
Biran completes one of the easy puzzles in 35 seconds.

Biran says he can complete all 10 of the easy puzzles in under
6 minutes.

Is Biran correct?
You must show all your calculations and write down any
assumptions you make.

(Total for Question 13 is 2 marks)

Turn to page 140 for complete worked solutions to the questions on this page.

14 The pie chart shows information about how the students in Year 11 get to school.

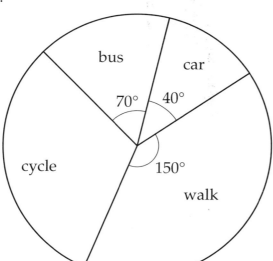

Mr Morley says: "Fewer than 10% of students in Year 11 get to school by car."

(a) Is Mr Morley correct?

You must explain your answer.

....

....

....

....

(2)

50 students in Year 11 cycle to school.

(b) How many students in Year 11 walk to school?

.... students

(3)

(Total for Question 14 is 5 marks)

PROBABILITY & STATISTICS

Revision Guide
Page 118

Hint

For part **(a)** you need to answer the question **and** explain your reason. Work out what angle 10% would represent, then write a conclusion.

Watch out!

Write units for degrees (°) in your working, so you don't get confused between the angles and the number of students.

LEARN IT!

The sectors in a pie chart add up to 360°.

Problem solved!

There are lots of steps for part **(b)** so **plan** your answer. You need to work out:

• the angle of the 'cycle' sector
• the angle each student represents
• the number of students who walk to school.

Turn to page 140 for complete worked solutions to the questions on this page.

Revision Guide
Page 19

Watch out!

Read the question carefully. You need to buy **exactly** 750 g, so work out the different combinations that allow you to do that.

Hint

Use letters to show each combination. You could write the combination 'five of can A' as 5A.

Problem solved!

Use a **systematic** method to make sure you have considered every possibility. Start by considering all the combinations that include can C. Then count the combinations that include cans A and B, and so on.

Hint

The amount you need is **not** a multiple of 100 g. This means that you have to include **at least one** of can A in every combination.

---

15 A shop sells tins of beans in three different sizes.

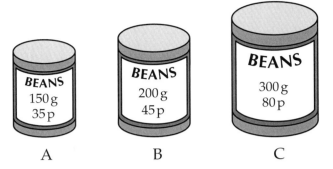

A   B   C

Kathy wants to buy exactly 750 g of beans.
She wants to buy the beans at the cheapest possible cost.

Work out the cheapest cost.
You must show all your working.

£ ....
(Total for Question 15 is 4 marks)

Turn to page 140 for complete worked solutions to the questions on this page.

16 Here is a knife.

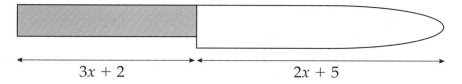

$$3x + 2 \qquad\qquad 2x + 5$$

All measurements are in centimetres.

The length of the handle is $3x + 2$
The length of the blade is $2x + 5$

The total length of the knife is 19 cm.

(a) Show that $5x + 7 = 19$

(1)

(b) Solve $5x + 7 = 19$

$x = $ ....
(2)
(Total for Question 16 is 3 marks)

 ALGEBRA

 Revision Guide Page 51

 Problem solved!

If you're not sure how to tackle this problem, try replacing the algebra with numbers. What operation would you do to find the total length of this knife?

←6 cm→←—9 cm—→

Now go back to the algebra version and try again.

Watch out!

When solving equations, the answer does not have to be a whole number.

ALGEBRA

 RATIO & PROPORTION

 Revision Guide Pages 40, 67

Watch out!

Convert all the distances into the same units before doing any calculations. You have been given two distances in miles, so it is easier to convert 240 km into miles.

Hint

The graph doesn't go up to 240 km, so you will have to convert a smaller length and then multiply. You could convert 24 km then multiply by 10, or convert 80 km then multiply by 3

Hint

Draw lines on your graph with a ruler and pencil to show any values you are reading off.

Explore

The gradient on this graph represents the number of miles in 1 km. Work out the gradient to complete this sentence:
1 km = ... miles

17 You can use this conversion graph to change between miles and kilometres.

Mary has to drive from Paris to Calais, and then from Dover to Sheffield.
The total distance she has to drive is 350 miles.

Mary has already driven 240 km from Paris to the ferry at Calais.
She goes on a ferry to Dover.
She now has to drive from Dover to Sheffield.

Mary has enough petrol to drive 180 miles.

Will Mary have to stop for petrol on the way to Sheffield?

(Total for Question 17 is 4 marks)

Turn to page 141 for complete worked solutions to the questions on this page.

18 (a) Find two factors of 36 with a difference of 5

.... and ....
(2)

The Lowest Common Multiple (LCM) of three numbers is 30
Two of the numbers are 2 and 5

(b) What could be the third number?

....
(2)
(Total for Question 18 is 4 marks)

NUMBER

Revision Guide
Pages 11, 12

Hint

For part **(a)**, start by writing all the factors of 36

LEARN IT!

The LCM of three numbers is the smallest number that is a multiple of all three numbers.

Problem solved!

There might be more than one possible answer. Read the question carefully. For part **(a)** you only need to give one pair of factors. For part **(b)** you only need to give one possible answer.

Turn to page 141 for complete worked solutions to the questions on this page.

35

PROBABILITY & STATISTICS

 Revision Guide
Page 123

Hint

The members of the group that took between 4 and 6 minutes would be plotted at 5 minutes on the horizontal axis. Read up from 5 and across to the vertical axis.

Hint

There were 25 friends in total, so write the value from the graph as a fraction over 25

Problem solved!

Always give **evidence** when you are comparing two distributions. For example, you could compare the number of friends who solved each puzzle in less than 2 minutes.

Watch out!

Don't waste time writing long answers. Compare values for each distribution, then write a short conclusion.

19 Zoe asked a group of 25 friends to complete two puzzles.

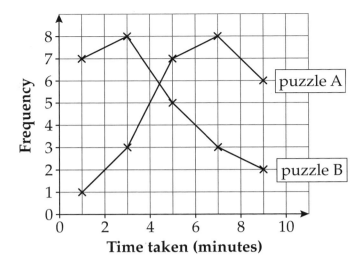

The frequency polygon shows the times taken by each of her 25 friends to complete each puzzle.

(a) Write down what fraction of the group took between 4 minutes and 6 minutes to complete puzzle **A**.

....
(2)

(b) Which puzzle was harder?
Give a reason for your answer.

....

....

....

(2)
(Total for Question 19 is 4 marks)

Turn to page 141 for complete worked solutions to the questions on this page.

20

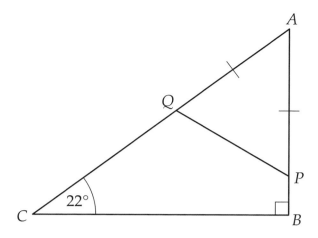

ABC is a right-angled triangle.
Angle *B* = 90°
Angle *ACB* = 22°

P is a point on *AB*.
Q is a point on *AC*.
AP = *AQ*

Work out the size of angle *APQ*.
Give reasons for each stage of your working.

°
....
(Total for Question 20 is 5 marks)

Turn to page 141 for complete worked solutions to the questions on this page.

37

Revision Guide
Pages 60, 61

21   140 children will be at a school sports day.
Lily is going to give a cup of orange drink to each of the 140 children.
She is going to put 200 millilitres of orange drink in each cup.

The orange drink is made from orange squash and water.
The orange squash and water are mixed in the ratio 1 : 9 by volume.

Orange squash is sold in bottles containing 750 millilitres.

Work out how many bottles of orange squash Lily needs to buy.
You must show all your working.

....

(Total for Question 21 is 4 marks)

Turn to page 142 for complete worked solutions to the questions on this page.

22

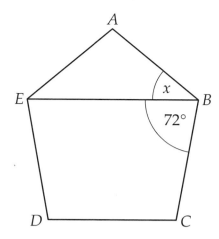

ABCDE is a regular polygon.
EB is a straight line.
Angle *EBC* = 72°

Work out the size of the angle marked *x*.

.... °

(Total for Question 22 is 3 marks)

 **GEOMETRY &
MEASURES**

Revision Guide
Pages 75, 76

Hint

You can answer lots of
questions about regular
polygons by finding the
size of one exterior
angle.

LEARN IT!

An exterior angle
in a regular *n*-sided
polygon is 360° ÷ *n*

Explore

You can divide a regular
pentagon up into three
triangles. The three
angles marked here are
all the same size:

Turn to page 142 for complete worked solutions to the questions on this page.

Revision Guide
Page 67

LEARN IT!

If *f* is inversely proportional to *d* then when you **multiply** *f* by a number you **divide** *d* by the same number.

Hint

If two quantities are inversely proportional then one gets smaller when the other one gets bigger. Your new value for *d* is bigger, so check that your new value for *f* is smaller.

Work out *d* × *f* for each pair of values. What do you notice?

23 *f* is inversely proportional to *d*.

When $d = 50, f = 256$

Find the value of *f* when $d = 80$

Scan this QR code for a video of this question being solved!

f = ...

(Total for Question 23 is 3 marks)

Turn to page 142 for complete worked solutions to the questions on this page.

24

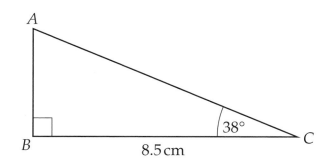

A

B

8.5 cm

38°

C

 GEOMETRY & MEASURES

 Revision Guide Page 93

The diagram shows triangle *ABC*.
BC = 8.5 cm
Angle *ABC* = 90°
Angle *ACB* = 38°

Work out the length of *AB*.
Give your answer correct to 3 significant figures.

LEARN IT!

Use S^O_H C^A_H T^O_A to remember the trigonometry formulae:

$$\sin = \frac{opp}{hyp}$$

$$\cos = \frac{adj}{hyp}$$

$$\tan = \frac{opp}{adj}$$

Hint

Label the sides of your triangle **relative to the angle** you know. *AB* is opposite the angle so label it 'opp'. The longest side is always the 'hyp'.

Watch out!

Make sure your calculator is in degrees mode.

Scan this QR code for a video of this question being solved!

..................................cm
(Total for Question 24 is 2 marks)

Turn to page 142 for complete worked solutions to the questions on this page.

GEOMETRY &
MEASURES

 Revision Guide
Page 103

LEARN IT!

Circumference =
π × diameter

Hint

Write down the formula for the circumference before you substitute.

Watch out!

Make sure you give answers to the right degree of accuracy. For part **(a)** you need to give your answer to the nearest centimetre. For part **(b)** you need to write down the number of **complete** turns.

Problem solved!

In part **(b)** you need to be careful with units. Make sure all your measurements are in the **same units** before doing any calculations.

25

The front wheel of Jared's bicycle has a diameter of 55 cm.

(a) Work out the circumference of Jared's front wheel.
Give your answer correct to the nearest centimetre.

..................................cm

(2)

Jared cycles 4.5 km to work each day.

(b) Work out the number of complete turns made by Jared's front wheel on his journey to work.

....

(2)

(Total for Question 25 is 4 marks)

Turn to page 143 for complete worked solutions to the questions on this page.

26 Henri and Ray buy some flowers for their mother.

They buy:
    2 bunches of roses and 3 bunches of tulips for £10
    1 bunch of roses and 4 bunches of tulips for £9.50.

(a) Work out the cost of one bunch of tulips.

£ ....
(4)

Henri is 16 years old and Ray is 2 years younger than Henri.

They share the total cost of £19.50 in the ratio of their ages.

(b) Work out how much Henri pays and how much Ray pays.

Henri £ ....

Ray £ ....
(3)

(Total for Question 26 is 7 marks)

TOTAL FOR PAPER IS 80 MARKS

Turn to page 143 for complete worked solutions to the questions on this page.

√xy² **ALGEBRA**

% **RATIO & PROPORTION**

Revision Guide
Pages 49, 60, 67

Problem solved!

For part **(a)** you will need to form two simultaneous equations and then solve them. Use *r* to represent the cost of one bunch of roses, and *t* to represent one bunch of tulips.

Hint

If you can't do the first part of a question you might still be able to do the second part. The first part needs algebra, but the second part is a ratio question.

Hint

Simplify the ratio before doing any calculations.

LEARN IT!

To divide a quantity in a given ratio:
- add together the parts in the ratio
- divide the amount by the total
- multiply the answer by each number of parts.

123 NUMBER

Revision Guide
Page 1

Hint

Compare tenths first,
then hundredths.

Revision Guide
Pages 7, 8, 16

Watch out!

You need to work
out the total in the
brackets **before** you
cube the number.

√xy² ALGEBRA

Revision Guide
Page 30

Hint

To **solve** an equation
you need to get the
letter on its own on one
side of the equation.
Make sure you apply the
same operation to both
sides of the equation at
each stage.

Paper 3: Calculator
Time allowed: 1 hour 30 minutes

1 Write the following numbers in order of size.
Start with the smallest number.

$$0.37 \qquad 0.3 \qquad 0.73 \qquad 0.307$$

0.3 , 0.37, 0.73, 0.307

(Total for Question 1 is 1 mark)

---

2 Find the value of $(3.4 + 0.12)^3$

3.4 + 0.12 = 3.52³ = 43.61

43.61

(Total for Question 2 is 1 mark)

---

3 (a) Solve $y \div 4 = 20$

$y =$ 80

(1)

(b) Solve $3x - 5 = 19$

+5 +5 = 24 ÷ 3 = 8

$x =$ 8

(2)

(Total for Question 3 is 3 marks)

Turn to page 144 for complete worked solutions to the questions on this page.

4 12 bags of cement cost £43.80.

Work out the cost of 17 bags of cement.

4z   43.80 ÷ 12 = 3.65

⁻3.65 ×17 = 62.05

£ 62.05

(Total for Question 4 is 2 marks)

Turn to page 144 for complete worked solutions to the questions on this page.

RATIO & PROPORTION

 Revision Guide
Pages 1, 67

Hint

Divide by 12 to find the cost of 1 bag of cement, then multiply by 17

Hint

Check that your answer makes sense. The total for 17 bags should be about one and half times as much as the amount for 12 bags.

Watch out!

Always give amounts in £ to two decimal places, even if the last digit is 0

Revision Guide
Page 1

Problem solved!

There are quite a few steps for this question. You are most likely to get a correct answer if you lay your working out neatly. Write words with your working to explain what you are working out at each stage.

Watch out!

The question asks for the amount of **change** you would get from £50, not the total cost.

5 Here is some information about the prices of four light switches.

single switch   58p
brass switch   £3.40
double switch   £5.55
dimmer switch   £7.82

Buy two of the same switches and get the second half price.

Martin buys:

3 brass switches
and 2 dimmer switches.

He pays with a £50 note.

How much change should he get?

$3.40 \times 3 = 10.2$

$7.82 \times 2 = 15.664$

$10.2 + 15.64 = 25.84$

$$\begin{array}{r} 50.00 \\ -\ 25.84 \\ \hline 24.16 \end{array}$$

£ 24.16

(Total for Question 5 is 3 marks)

Turn to page 144 for complete worked solutions to the questions on this page.

6   Jim sells televisions.
He keeps a record of the number of televisions he sells each week.

The table gives some information about the number of each make of television he sold last week.

	Make of television		
	Sandi	**Bish**	**Ebo**
Monday	4	2	1
Tuesday	3	4	2
Wednesday	0	3	1
Thursday	0	5	2
Friday	1	1	1
Saturday	4	5	3

Jim's shop is closed on Sunday.

The table below gives information about the cost of each television.

	Make of television		
	Sandi	**Bish**	**Ebo**
Cost	£129	£149	£169

Jim is paid a bonus when all the televisions he sells in a week have a total cost of £6000 or more.

Will Jim be paid a bonus for last week?

$$Sandi = 4+3+0+0+1+4 = 12$$
$$Bish = 2+4+3+5+1+5 = 20$$
$$Ebo = 1+2+1+2+1+3 = 10$$

$$Sandi = 12 \times £129 = £1548$$
$$Bish = 20 \times £149 = £2980$$
$$Ebo = 10 \times £169 = £1690$$

$$1548 + 2980 + 1690 = £6218$$

yes because he sold over £6000 with of Tv.

(Total for Question 6 is 4 marks)

Turn to page 144 for complete worked solutions to the questions on this page.

NUMBER

Revision Guide Page 1

Hint

There are no complicated calculations here, but you have to work **neatly** and keep track of your working.

Problem solved!

Start by adding up the number of each make of television he sold in the whole week. Then you only have to do 3 calculations rather than 18!

Watch out!

You need to answer the question, **and** show enough working to justify your answer.

Revision Guide
Pages 79, 80

LEARN IT!

Area of trapezium
$= \frac{1}{2}(a + b)h$

Problem solved!

Plan your strategy before you start. Here are two options:

1. Work out the area of all four pieces, then divide by 4

2. Find the dimensions of one piece, then use the formula for the area of a trapezium.

Hint

You can use any strategy you like, but you must show your working.

7 Jake makes a picture frame from 4 identical pieces of card.
Each piece of card is in the shape of a trapezium.

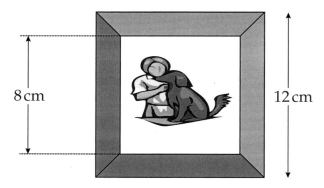

8 cm   12 cm

The outer edge of the frame is a square of side 12 cm.
The inner edge of the frame is a square of side 8 cm.

Work out the area of each piece of card.

Area of 4 pieces $= 12^2 - 8^2$

$= 144 - 64$

$= 80$

$80 \div 4 = 20$

Scan this QR code for a video of this question being solved!

20 cm^2 .... cm²

(Total for Question 7 is 4 marks)

Turn to page 145 for complete worked solutions to the questions on this page.

8   Jane helps to organise a dance group.
The dancers use sticks in some of the dances.

Jane needs some ribbon to tie on the sticks.
She needs to buy enough ribbon for 20 sticks.

Each stick has 8 pieces of ribbon.
Each piece of ribbon is 30 cm long.

The ribbon is sold in rolls.
Each roll has 25 m of ribbon.

How many rolls of ribbon does Jane need to buy?

....
(Total for Question 8 is 3 marks)

NUMBER

Revision Guide
Page 1

Problem solved!

Work out the length
of ribbon needed for 1
stick, then calculate the
total length of ribbon
needed for 20 sticks.

LEARN IT!

1 m = 100 cm, so divide
cm by 100 to convert
to metres.

Hint

Make sure your answer
makes sense. It's
unlikely that Jane would
need to buy hundreds
of rolls!

Watch out!

Jane needs to buy a
whole number of rolls.

Turn to page 145 for complete worked solutions to the questions on this page.

ALGEBRA

 Revision Guide
Page 51

Problem solved!

Plan your strategy before you start. Here are two possible strategies for this question:

1. Write the number as *x*, then form an equation. Solve your equation to find the value of *x*.

2. Draw function machines showing James' operations. Work backwards to find the number.

Watch out!

Don't just try numbers. You might waste a lot of time.

Hint

You should always **check** your answer for questions like this. Multiply your answer by 8 then add 7. You should get 89

9 James thinks of a number.

He multiplies his number by 8
He subtracts 7 from the result.

His answer is 89

What number did James think of?

$$89 + 7 \div 8 = 12$$

Scan this QR code for a video of this question being solved!

....

(Total for Question 9 is 2 marks)

Turn to page 145 for complete worked solutions to the questions on this page.

10 Mike is a school caretaker.
He is marking out the positions of some posts in the school yard.

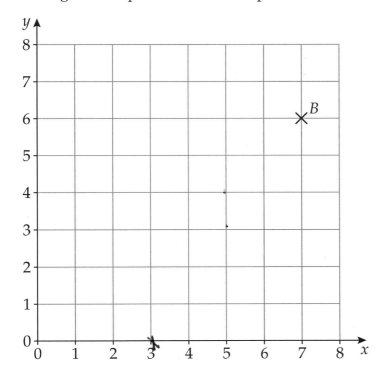

The cross at *B* shows the position for a basketball post.

Mike is going to put a netball post at the point (3, 0).

Mike wants to paint a spot on the yard exactly halfway between the two posts.

Work out the coordinates of the position of the spot.

(...........5.........., ...43........)

(Total for Question 10 is 2 marks)

Turn to page 145 for complete worked solutions to the questions on this page.

√xy² ALGEBRA

Revision Guide Page 36

LEARN IT!

To find the **midpoint** of two points, add the *x*-coordinates and divide by 2, and add the *y*-coordinates and divide by 2

Problem solved!

You can probably solve this problem **by drawing a diagram**. Plot the position of the netball post, then join the two points. Work out the coordinates of the point in the middle of this line.

Hint

A coordinate grid is an accurate drawing, so you could even work out the midpoint by **measuring**.

ALGEBRA

 Revision Guide Page 26

11 This formula is used to work out the body mass index, B, for a person of mass M kg and height H metres.

$$B = \frac{M}{H^2}$$

A person with a body mass index between 25 and 30 is overweight.

Arthur has a mass of 96 kg.
He has a height of 2 metres.

Is Arthur overweight?
You must show all your working.

$$\frac{96}{2^2} = 24$$

(Total for Question 11 is 3 marks)

Turn to page 146 for complete worked solutions to the questions on this page.

12 Gary recorded the number of eggs in each of 10 nests.
Here are his results.

   1   1   2   2   2   2   3   3   3   4

(a) Write down the mode.

.... 2 ....

(1)

(b) Work out the mean.

$$1 + 1 + 2 + 2 + 2 + 2 + 2 + 3 + 3 + 3 + 4 = 23 \div 10$$

.... 2 2.3 ....

(2)

(c) Which best describes the average numbers of eggs in these nests, the mode or the mean?
Give a reason for your answer.

....

....

....

(1)

(Total for Question 12 is 4 marks)

PROBABILITY & STATISTICS

 Revision Guide Page 120

Hint

The mode is the most commonly occurring value. Make sure you write down the **data value** and not the number of times it appears in the list.

LEARN IT!

To find the mean, add up the data values then divide by the number of data values.

Watch out!

For part **(c)** you **must** give a reason. Choose one of the averages, and then explain why you chose it.

Explore

When the news talks about 'average' salaries, they are usually referring to the **median**. Mean income can be misleading because it is affected by a small number of people who earn a lot of money.

Turn to page 146 for complete worked solutions to the questions on this page.

53

RATIO &
PROPORTION

Foundation
Pages 57, 63

Problem solved!

Work out Colin's total profit in 2013. Increase this amount by 40% and compare the result to Colin's total profit in 2014. Write a short conclusion.

Hint

The multiplier for a 40% increase is × 1.4

Hint

For part **(b)**, look at the difference between Colin's 2013 and 2014 profits. How do you think Colin has reached his estimate?

Explore

You could make a better estimate for Colin's 2015 profit using percentage increases. Work out his percentage increase in profits from 2013 to 2014, then increase his 2014 profit by that amount.

13 Colin makes and sells chocolates.
Here is information about his profits for the past two years.

	Jan–Jun	Jul–Dec
2013	£5000	£5400
2014	£5600	£7800

Colin writes this statement in his report:
'My total profit in 2014 is 40% more than my total profit in 2013'.

(a) Is this statement correct?
You must show all your working.

$5000 + 5400 = 10400$

$5600 + 7800 = 13400$

no   40% more   would   be 14560

not   13400

(3)

Colin says that in 2015 he should make a total profit of £16 400

(b) What assumptions has Colin made?

(1)

(Total for Question 13 is 4 marks)

Turn to page 146 for complete worked solutions to the questions on this page.

14

A, B, C and D are points on a straight line.
$AD = 40\,$cm
$AB = 8\,$cm
$BC = CD$

Explain why $AB : CD = 1 : 2$

(Total for Question 14 is 4 marks)

RATIO & PROPORTION

Revision Guide
Page 59

Hint

Start by working out
the length of CD.

Watch out!

The diagram is not
drawn accurately, so
you can't measure. Use
the information given in
the question to work
out any missing lengths.

Problem solved!

When a question
says "Explain…" you
need to show all your
working clearly. Write
down what you are
calculating at each
stage.

Turn to page 146 for complete worked solutions to the questions on this page.

55

GEOMETRY & MEASURES

 Revision Guide Pages 72, 75

LEARN IT!

Squares have **equal sides** and **right angles**. You might need to use quadrilateral facts in an angles question.

Hint

Unless it says so in the question, the diagram is **not accurate**. Don't measure the size of the angle – work it out using angle facts.

Watch out!

Check that your answer makes sense. The missing angle is **obtuse** so your answer should be between 90° and 180°

15

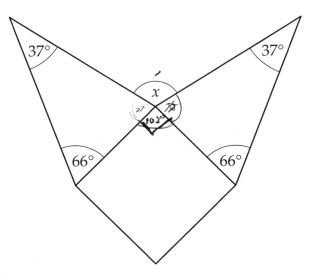

The diagram shows two congruent triangles and a square.
Find the size of the angle marked x.

$37 + 66 = \text{to}3$

$180 - 103 = 77$

$77 + 77 \neq 153$

$153 - 363 - 266$

$154 + 90 =$

244
380
294
$\overline{116}$

$x = \underline{\quad 116° \quad}$ °

(Total for Question 15 is 3 marks)

Turn to page 147 for complete worked solutions to the questions on this page.

16 You can use this conversion to change between pounds (£) and dollars ($).

$$£25 = \$40$$

Stacey bought a watch in New York.
The watch cost $220

In London, the same type of watch costs £140

Compare the cost of the watch in New York with the cost of the watch in London.

$$\cancel{40} \quad 220 \div 40 = 5.5$$

$$25 \times 5.5 = 137.5 \text{ -new york}$$

$$140 - 137.5$$

$$\cancel{140}$$

$$140 - 137.5 = 2.5$$

(Total for Question 16 is 3 marks)

 Revision Guide
Page 67

Problem solved!

You can only compare quantities when they are in the same units. Convert $220 into £ or convert £140 into $.

Hint

To convert from $ to £ divide the amount by 40, then multiply by 25. Remember to show all your working.

Watch out!

You need to write a short **conclusion** comparing the costs. You can use < or > to show which cost is higher.

 Explore

Write this exchange rate in the form:

£1 = $..........................

$1 = £..........................

Turn to page 147 for complete worked solutions to the questions on this page.

PROBABILITY & STATISTICS

Revision Guide
Page 131

LEARN IT!

At each branch the probabilities add up to 1

Hint

You only need to complete the spaces marked with dotted lines. You don't need to work out the probabilities of the final outcomes.

Hint

Kelvin and Mamady's arrival times are **independent events** – the outcome of one does not affect the probabilities of the other. This means that both sets of branches for Mamady have the same probabilities.

17 Kelvin and Mamady are in the same class.
The probability that Kelvin arrives on time is 0.7
The probability that Mamady arrives on time is 0.9

Complete the probability tree diagram.

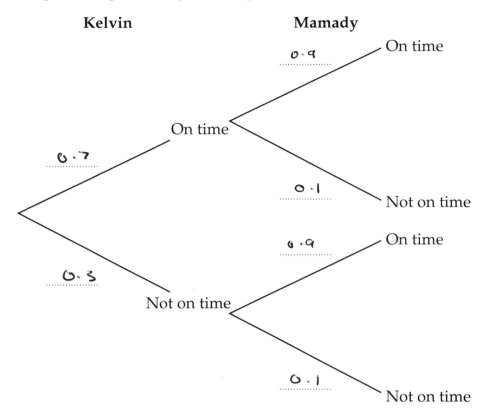

Kelvin   Mamady

0.9 — On time
0.7 — On time
0.1 — Not on time
0.3 — Not on time
0.9 — On time
0.1 — Not on time

(Total for Question 17 is 2 marks)

Turn to page 147 for complete worked solutions to the questions on this page.

18 £360 is shared in the ratio 1 : 3 : 5

Work out the difference between the largest share and the smallest share.

$$1 + 3 + 5 = 9$$

$$360 \div 9 = 40$$

$$1 \times 40 = 40$$
$$3 \times 40 = 120$$
$$\cancel{3}5 \times 40 = 200$$

$$40 : 120 : 200$$

£ 160

(Total for Question 18 is 3 marks)

% RATIO & PROPORTION

 Revision Guide Page 60

Hint

You can solve lots of ratio problems by working out what **one part** of the ratio is worth. There are 1 + 3 + 5 = 9 parts in the ratio in total.

Watch out!

The question asks you to find the **difference** between the largest and the smallest shares.

Turn to page 147 for complete worked solutions to the questions on this page.

PROBABILITY & STATISTICS

Revision Guide
Pages 124, 127

Problem solved!

Always give **evidence** when you are comparing two distributions. Try to compare one average and one measure of spread. Make sure your statements refer to the **context** of the question. You need to talk about **heights**.

Hint

For back-to-back stem-and-leaf diagrams, you should compare the **range** and the **median**.

Watch out!

When reading data values from a stem-and-leaf diagram, make sure you use the full data value, not just the 'leaf'.

Watch out!

Don't waste time writing long-winded answers. Compare values for each distribution, then write a short conclusion.

---

19 The heights (in cm) of 13 girls and 13 boys were recorded.

The back-to-back stem-and-leaf diagram gives this information.

				girls		boys				
			9	8	14					
			4	2	15	7	9			
8	4	4	2	0	16	2	6	8	9	
	9	5	3	0	17	0	3	4	6	6
					18	1	4			

KEY:

8 | 14 represents a height of 148 cm for girls

15 | 7 represents a height of 157 cm for boys

Compare the distribution of the heights of the girls and the distribution of the heights of the boys.

(Total for Question 19 is 3 marks)

Turn to page 148 for complete worked solutions to the questions on this page.

20 A number is increased by 25% to get 5950

What is the number?

$5950 \div 125 = 47.6 \times 100$

4760

4760

....

(Total for Question 20 is 3 marks)

Turn to page 148 for complete worked solutions to the questions on this page.

% RATIO & PROPORTION

Revision Guide
Page 62

Watch out!

This is a **reverse percentages** question. You are given the amount **after** the increase, and you need to find the **original amount**.

Hint

Here are two possible strategies:
1. Find the multiplier for a 25% increase, then **divide** 5950 by the multiplier.
2. Divide 5950 by 125 to find 1%, then multiply by 100 to find 100%.

Hint

Increase your answer by 25% and **check** that you get 5950

Revision Guide
Pages 1, 61, 67

LEARN IT!

1 kg = 1000 g

Watch out!

Convert measurements into the same units before carrying out any calculations.

Problem solved!

Work out how many batches of the recipe Rosie can make.
You need to do the calculations for **all** the ingredients, then choose the **smallest** number of batches.

Explore

The official definition of a kilogram has changed through history. In 1795, 1 kg was defined as the mass of 1 litre of water at 0 °C. The definition is now based on the mass of a platinum alloy block which is stored near Paris.

21 Here is a list of ingredients for making small cakes.

Small cakes
400 g   flour
200 g   butter
200 g   sugar
2   eggs
Makes 15 small cakes

Rosie has

2 kg	of flour
800 g	of butter
1.5 kg	of sugar
12	eggs

What is the greatest number of small cakes Rosie can make?

You must show all your working.

....
(Total for Question 21 is 4 marks)

Turn to page 148 for complete worked solutions to the questions on this page.

22 Savio has two fair dice.
    He throws the two dice and adds the scores together.

    (a) What is the probability of getting a total of exactly 11?

    ....

    (3)

    (b) What total score is Savio most likely to get?

    ....

    (1)

    Savio says:

    "The probability of getting a total of 5 or more is $\frac{3}{4}$."

    (c) Is Savio correct?
        You must show your working.

    ....

    (2)
    (Total for Question 22 is 6 marks)

Turn to page 148 for complete worked solutions to the questions on this page.

PROBABILITY & STATISTICS

Revision Guide
Pages 131, 133

Hint

You can show all the possible outcomes for the total when two dice are thrown by drawing a sample space diagram. There are 36 possible outcomes in total.

LEARN IT!

To find a probability, count the number of **successful outcomes** and divide by the total number of possible outcomes.

Explore

There is only one way of scoring a total of 2 on two dice, but there are six different ways of scoring a 7. This is why you are more likely to score 7

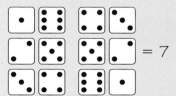

Find another score that is as likely as a total of 2. Is there another score that is as likely as a total of 7?

Revision Guide
Page 44

23 (a) Complete the table of values for $y = x^2 - 3x + 1$

x	-1	0	1	2	3	4
y	....	1	....	....	1	5

(2)

(b) Draw the graph of $y = x^2 - 3x + 1$ for values of x from -1 to 4

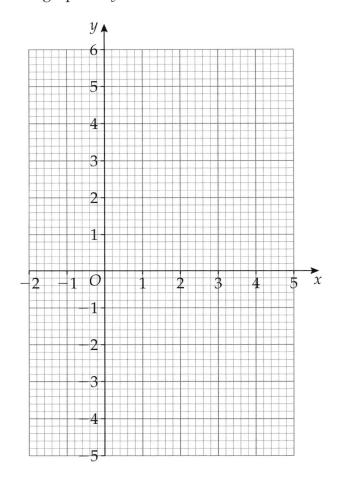

(2)

(Total for Question 23 is 4 marks)

Turn to page 149 for complete worked solutions to the questions on this page.

24 Caroline is making some table decorations.
Each decoration is made from a candle
and a holder.

Caroline buys some candles and some
holders each in packs.

There are 30 candles in a pack of candles.
There are 18 holders in a pack of holders.

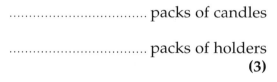

candle and
holder

Caroline buys exactly the same number of
candles and holders.

(a) What is the smallest number of packs of candles and holders
that Caroline can buy?

.... packs of candles

.... packs of holders
(3)

Caroline uses all her candles and all her holders.

(b) How many table decorations does Caroline make?

.... table decorations
(1)
(Total for Question 24 is 4 marks)

NUMBER

 Revision Guide
Page 12

Hint

The number of candles
must be a multiple
of 30. The number
of holders must be a
multiple of 18. So you
need to find the LCM
of 30 and 18

Watch out!

Caroline buys the same
number of candles
and holders. But she
doesn't buy the same
number of packs.

Problem solved!

Keep track of your
working. You could
draw a table showing
the number of candles
and holders for
different numbers of
packs. Circle the first
numbers that match,
and remember to write
the number of **packs**
as your answer.

Turn to page 149 for complete worked solutions to the questions on this page.

Revision Guide
Page 47

Hint

You need to find two numbers that **add up to −2** and **multiply to give −24**. One must be positive and one must be negative.

Watch out!

This quadratic equation has **two solutions**. Write your answer as '$x = \square$ or $x = \square$'.

 Revision Guide
Page 112

LEARN IT!

When you multiply a vector by a number you multiply **both parts** by that number:

$$3\begin{pmatrix} 5 \\ -1 \end{pmatrix} = \begin{pmatrix} 15 \\ -3 \end{pmatrix}$$

LEARN IT!

When you add or subtract vectors you add or subtract **both parts**.

Explore

$a - 3b$ means that you travel along a, then travel **backwards** along b three times.

---

25 Solve $x^2 - 2x - 24 = 0$

Scan this QR code for a video of this question being solved!

(Total for Question 25 is 3 marks)

26 $a = \begin{pmatrix} -3 \\ -2 \end{pmatrix}$ $b = \begin{pmatrix} 5 \\ -1 \end{pmatrix}$

Work out $a - 3b$ as a column vector

(Total for Question 26 is 2 marks)

TOTAL FOR PAPER IS 80 MARKS

Turn to page 149 for complete worked solutions to the questions on this page.

Paper 1: Non-calculator
Time allowed: 1 hour 30 minutes

1   (a)   There were 5781 people at a football match.

Write down the value of the 8 in the number 5781

....
(1)

(b)   The length of a nail is 1.76 cm.

Write down the value of the 7 in 1.76

....
(1)
(Total for Question 1 is 2 marks)

2   (a)   Annabel's thumb is 2.5 centimetres long.

Change 2.5 centimetres to millimetres.

..................................mm
(1)

(b)   There are 450 millilitres of water in a jug.

Change 450 millilitres to litres.

..................................litres
(1)
(Total for Question 2 is 2 marks)

Turn to page 150 for complete worked solutions to the questions on this page.

NUMBER

Revision Guide
Page 1

Hint

Ten thousands	Thousands	Hundreds	Tens	Units
5	7	8	1	

Hint

You can write your answer in words or numbers. The 7 is **after** the decimal point so it is worth **less** than 1

RATIO AND PROPORTION

Revision Guide
Page 61

Hint

mm are smaller than cm, so to convert from cm to mm you **multiply** by 10

LEARN IT!

There are 1000 ml in 1 litre.

Revision Guide
Page 1

Hint

When you divide by
1000 the digits move
three places to the
right on a place-value
diagram.

Revision Guide
Page 11

Problem solved!

Start by writing out
a list of all the prime
numbers up to 20

Watch out!

Read the question
carefully. You need
to find four **different**
prime numbers.

---

3 Write down $\frac{23}{1000}$ as a decimal.

....

(Total for Question 3 is 1 mark)

---

4 Find four different prime numbers you can add together to get a
number greater than 30 and less than 40

....

(Total for Question 4 is 2 marks)

  Turn to page 150 for complete worked solutions to the questions on this page.

5 Mary buys three tickets for a theatre show.
Each ticket costs £49.50 plus booking fee.

The booking fee is £2.25 per ticket.

Mary has £150 in her purse.

Does she have enough money to pay for the total cost of the tickets?

Scan this QR
code for a video
of this question
being solved!

(Total for Question 5 is 3 marks)

ALGEBRA

 Revision Guide
Page 25

LEARN IT!

Use **BIDMAS** to remember the correct order of operations:

Brackets
Indices
Division
Multiplication
Addition
Subtraction

Hint

Use brackets when substituting a negative number.
$(-6)^2 = -6 \times -6$
$\qquad = 36$

6 $K = 3h^2 - j$

   $h = -6$

   $j = 8$

   Work out the value of K.

$K =$ ....
(Total for Question 6 is 2 marks)

Turn to page 150 for complete worked solutions to the questions on this page.

7 A company sells toy cars.
The company has 5 cars left to sell.

2 of the cars are blue.
3 of the cars are red.

Carl buys a toy car.
The company picks the toy car at random.

(a) On the probability scale, mark with a cross (×) the probability
that Carl gets a yellow car.

(1)

(b) On the probability scale, mark with a cross (×) the probability
that Carl gets a blue car.

(1)

(c) There are some boys and girls in a nursery.

The probability of choosing a girl at random is $\frac{4}{7}$

What is the probabilty of choosing a boy?

....
(1)

(Total for Question 7 is 3 marks)

Turn to page 151 for complete worked solutions to the questions on this page.

PROBABILITY & STATISTICS

Revision Guide
Page 128

Hint

A probability scale
goes from 0 to 1. 0 is
'impossible' and 1 is
'certain'.

LEARN IT!

Probability =

$\frac{\text{Number of successful outcomes}}{\text{Total number of possible outcomes}}$

Hint

2 out of 5 of the cars
are blue. Write this as a
fraction, then work out
where it goes on the
probability scale.

Explore

Can you describe the
probablities in words?
Choose one of these
options:

| Impossible |
| Very unlikely |
| Unlikely |
| Even chance |
| Likely |
| Very likely |
| Certain |

Revision Guide
Page 1

Problem solved!

Solve this problem one step at a time:

1. Find Jim's normal rate of pay.

2. Work out how much he earns on Saturday and Sunday.

3. Add these amounts to £400

4. Write a conclusion.

Hint

You need to do 400 ÷ 25 to find Jim's normal rate of pay. You can simplify this division by multiplying both numbers by 4

Hint

To multiply a number by 1.5 find half of the number then add it on.

8   Jim is an IT consultant.

Jim is paid at his normal rate of pay from Monday to Friday.
On a Saturday he is paid 1.5 times his normal rate.
On a Sunday he is paid twice his normal rate.

One week he works 7 days for a company.
He is paid £400 for 25 hours of work from Monday to Friday.
He works for 6 hours on Saturday.
He works for 3 hours on Sunday.

Does he earn enough money this week to pay for a deposit of £650 for a car?
You must show all your working.

(Total for Question 8 is 5 marks)

Turn to page 151 for complete worked solutions to the questions on this page.

9 David takes, at random, a number from Box A.
He then takes, at random, a letter from Box B.

Box A   **Box B**

Box A:
1
     2
   6

Box B:
A
   C
       E

(a) List all the possible outcomes he could get.

....

....

....

                                                                                      (2)

(b) Find the probability that David takes the number 2 and the
letter E.

....

                                                                                        (1)

(c) Find the probability that David picks the letter C.

....

                                                                                        (1)

(Total for Question 9 is 4 marks)

NUMBER

PROBABILITY & STATISTICS

Revision Guide
Pages 19, 131

Problem solved!

Use a **systematic** approach to make sure you have listed every possible outcome. You could start by listing all the combinations that include the number 1, and so on.

Hint

There should be 9 possible outcomes in total.

Hint

For part **(b)**, only one outcome contains the number 2 and the letter E. Each outcome is equally likely so divide 1 by the total number of possible outcomes.

Explore

The probability that David takes the number 2 or the letter E is $\frac{5}{9}$. Can you see why?

ALGEBRA

 Revision Guide
Pages 34, 35

Problem solved!

The easiest way to solve this problem is to continue the sequence and see if 34 is a term.

Watch out!

If 34 is not a term in the sequence, make sure you write down at least one term larger than 34

 Explore

You could also solve this problem by finding the *n*th term in the sequence. The term-to-term rule is 'add 3' so the *n*th term will look like $3n + \square$ or $3n - \square$.

10 Here are the first four terms in a number sequence.

    5   8   11   14

Kasey thinks that the number 34 is in this sequence.

Is Kasey correct?
You must show how you get your answer.

(Total for Question 10 is 2 marks)

Turn to page 151 for complete worked solutions to the questions on this page.

11 Which of these fractions is the larger?

$\frac{1}{3}$ or $\frac{2}{5}$

You must show clearly how you got your answer.

(Total for Question 11 is 2 marks)

 NUMBER

Revision Guide
Page 13

Hint

To **compare** two fractions you need to find equivalent fractions with the same denominator. You can use a denominator of 15 for this question:

LEARN IT!

You can find equivalent fractions by multiplying or dividing the numerator and denominator by the same number.

Problem solved!

You need to work out which fraction is larger. **Show your working,** then write a short **conclusion**.

Turn to page 152 for complete worked solutions to the questions on this page.

75

GEOMETRY & MEASURES

Revision Guide
Pages 95, 96, 98

Hint

Use a protractor to draw a 60° angle at B. You need to measure your angle accurate to the nearest degree.

Hint

Then use a ruler to mark a point 6 cm along that line from B. Measure lines accurate to the nearest mm. Join your mark to A using your ruler.

Watch out!

Always use a **sharp pencil** for any constructions in your exam. Don't rub out any of your construction marks or lines.

 Explore

Use your scale drawing to work out the real-life distance from A to C.

---

12 Here is the sketch of a garden.

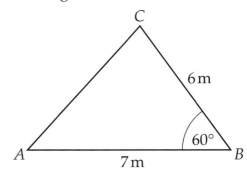

Draw an accurate diagram of the garden.
Use a scale of 1 cm represents 1 m.
The side *AB* has already been drawn for you.

A   *B*

(Total for Question 12 is 2 marks)

Turn to page 152 for complete worked solutions to the questions on this page.

13 Sherri says:

"If you multiply an odd number by 7 and take away 2, you always get a prime number."

Show that Sherri is wrong.

(Total for Question 13 is 2 marks)

¹²³ **NUMBER**

√xy² **ALGEBRA**

Revision Guide Pages 11, 52

Hint

You only need one **counter-example** to show that Sherri is wrong.

LEARN IT!

Learn the prime numbers below 50. Here are the first few: 2, 3, 5, 7, 11, 13, 17…

Problem solved!

Try some different odd numbers. Multiply them by 7 and take away 2. Write down your working carefully. When you find one that doesn't give a prime number, write a conclusion.

Turn to page 152 for complete worked solutions to the questions on this page.

Revision Guide
Page 56

Hint

To compare fractions, decimals and percentages convert them all into the same type. There are two decimals, so convert $\frac{2}{3}$ and 65% to decimals.

LEARN IT!

The fractions $\frac{1}{3}$ and $\frac{2}{3}$ produce **recurring decimals**.

$\frac{1}{3}$ = 0.3333...

$\frac{2}{3}$ = 0.6666...

LEARN IT!

To convert a percentage into a decimal you divide by 100

14 Write these numbers in order of size.
Start with the smallest number.

$$0.6 \qquad \frac{2}{3} \qquad 65\% \qquad 0.606$$

....

(Total for Question 14 is 2 marks)

Turn to page 152 for complete worked solutions to the questions on this page.

15

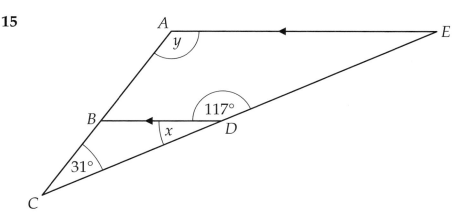

AE is parallel to BD.
ABC and CDE are straight lines.

(a) (i) Work out the size of the angle marked x.

x = ...°
(1)

(ii) Give a reason for your answer.

....

....
(1)

(b) (i) Work out the size of the angle marked y.

y = ...°

(ii) Give the reasons for your answer.

....

....
(3)
(Total for Question 15 is 5 marks)

**GEOMETRY &
MEASURES**

Revision Guide
Pages 73, 74

LEARN IT!

Angles on a straight
line add up to 180°

LEARN IT!

Angles in a triangle
add up to 180°

LEARN IT!

Corresponding angles
on parallel lines are
equal.

Hint

If you know two angles
in a triangle, add them
together, then subtract
the result from 180°.
This will give you the
third angle in the
triangle.

Revision Guide
Page 98

Hint

Read the scale carefully. Each metre in real life is represented by 2.5 cm on the model.

Hint

Write down the calculation you use as well as your final answer.

Watch out!

Make sure your answers make sense.

Explore

If you want to write this scale as a ratio you need to make sure both parts are in the same units. 1 m = 100 cm so the ratio is 100 : 2.5

16

A model of a space shuttle is made to a scale of 2.5 centimetres to 1 metre.
The length of the space shuttle is 30 metres.

(a) Work out the length of the model.
Give your answer in centimetres.

.... cm
(2)

The height of the model is 12.5 centimetres.

(b) Work out the height of the space shuttle.
Give your answer in metres.

.... m
(2)

(Total for Question 16 is 4 marks)

Turn to page 153 for complete worked solutions to the questions on this page.

17 A machine makes 36 trophies every hour.

The machine makes trophies for $8\frac{1}{2}$ hours each day, on 5 days of the week.

The trophies are packed into boxes.
Each box holds 8 trophies.

How many boxes are needed for all the trophies made each week?

.... boxes
(Total for Question 17 is 4 marks)

18 Expand and simplify

$(x + 4)(x + 6)$

....
(Total for Question 18 is 2 marks)

Turn to page 153 for complete worked solutions to the questions on this page.

 NUMBER

 Revision Guide
Pages 5, 15

Hint

Calculate $36 \times 8\frac{1}{2}$ to find how many trophies are made each day.

Use a written or mental method to find 36×8, then add on half of 36.

Then multiply the result by 5 to work out how many are made each week.

Divide the number of trophies made each week by 8. You need to fit all the trophies into boxes, so round up to the next whole number.

Explore

Can you describe a mental method for working out 36×8?

 ALGEBRA

 Revision Guide
Page 43

Hint

You can use a grid to expand double brackets:

	x	+4
x		+4*x*
+6		

Complete all four terms then add them together.

PROBABILITY & STATISTICS

 Revision Guide
Pages 128, 132

Hint

Your blank Venn diagram should look like this:

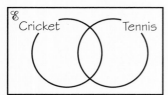

Hint

You know that 15 members play both sports, so you can write '15' in the centre of your Venn diagram.

Hint

Always check a Venn diagram by adding up all the numbers. The total should be 80

Watch out!

You don't need to simplify fractions when giving answers to probability questions.

Explore

How would the Venn diagram look if:
- no members played both sports
- every member who played tennis also played cricket?

---

19 Here is some information about a cricket and tennis club.

80 people belong to the club.
35 play cricket.
50 play tennis.
15 play both cricket and tennis.

(a) Draw a Venn diagram to show this information.

(4)

One of the people who belongs to the club is chosen at random.

(b) Work out the probability that this person does not play cricket or tennis.

....

(2)

(Total for Question 19 is 6 marks)

Turn to page 153 for complete worked solutions to the questions on this page.

20 Mark works for 5 days each week.

Mark can travel to work by car or train.

> **By car**
>
> He travels a total distance of 24 miles each day
>
> His car travels 30 miles per gallon
>
> Diesel costs £1.50 per litre

> **By train**
>
> Weekly pass costs £25.75

1 gallon = 4.5 litres

Is it more expensive if he uses his car or the train?

You must show your working.

**RATIO &
PROPORTION**

Revision Guide
Pages 1, 67

Problem solved!

Write words with your
working to explain what
you are working out at
each stage.

Hint

Use mental strategies
to save time. The total
distance Mark drives
in one week is 5 × 24
= 5 × 20 + 5 × 4 =
100 + 20 = 120 miles.

Hint

You need to work out
the total cost of the
diesel Mark would
use in one week. Then
compare this with the
cost of the weekly
train pass and write a
conclusion.

Hint

If you need to convert
between metric units
(like litres) and imperial
units (like gallons) in
your exam, you will be
given the conversion
with the question.

(Total for Question 20 is 4 marks)

Turn to page 154 for complete worked solutions to the questions on this page.

$\sqrt{xy^2}$ **ALGEBRA**

Revision Guide
Pages 45, 48

Hint

To complete the table, substitute each value of x into the right-hand side of the equation and work out the corresponding value of y.

Watch out!

When you cube a negative number the answer is negative:
$(-3)^3 = -3 \times -3 \times -3$
$\qquad = -27$

Hint

This is an example of a **cubic graph**. The graph should be a smooth curve. If one of your points doesn't follow the pattern check your working.

Watch out!

These solutions are based on reading off a graph. The accuracy of the solutions will depend on the accuracy of your graph.

21 (a) Complete the table of values for $y = x^3 - 4x$

x	-3	-2	-1	0	1	2	3
y			3	0			15

(2)

(b) On the grid, draw the graph of $y = x^3 - 4x$ from $x = -3$ to $x = 3$

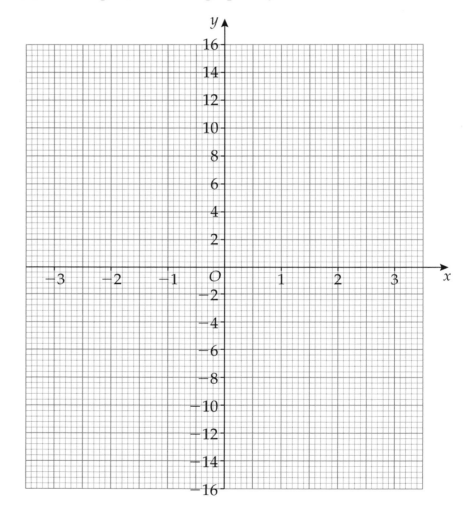

(2)

(c) Use your graph to find estimates of the solutions to the equation
$x^3 - 4x = 2$

....

(2)

(Total for Question 21 is 6 marks)

Turn to page 154 for complete worked solutions to the questions on this page.

22 Jean makes a metal structure out of steel rope.

The diagram below shows the metal structure.

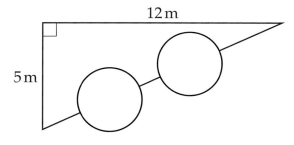

The two circles are identical.

The diameter of each circle is 2.5 metres.

Show that the total length of the steel rope used to make the metal structure is ($a + b\pi$) metres where a and b are integers.

(Total for Question 22 is 5 marks)

Revision Guide Pages 90, 103, 106

LEARN IT!

Use Pythagoras' theorem to find the length of the diagonal:

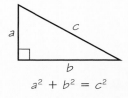

$a^2 + b^2 = c^2$

LEARN IT!

You need to know the square numbers up to 15^2, and their corresponding square roots.

LEARN IT!

Circumference = $\pi \times$ diameter

Hint

You can add together multiples of π. Each circle has circumference 2.5π so the total amount of wire needed for both circles is $2.5\pi + 2.5\pi = 5\pi$

Turn to page 154 for complete worked solutions to the questions on this page.

85

√xy² **ALGEBRA**

GEOMETRY & MEASURES

Revision Guide
Pages 22, 51, 74

Hint

$d + e + f = 180°$

Hint

You need to simplify your expression by collecting like terms. Group the y terms and the number terms.

Hint

If you can't work out a calculation for an equation mentally, use jottings. Write any workings neatly near your equation.

23

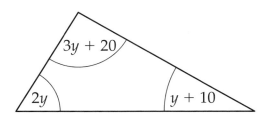

Find y.

Scan this QR code for a video of this question being solved!

$y =$ .... °

(3)

(Total for Question 23 is 3 marks)

Turn to page 154 for complete worked solutions to the questions on this page.

24 Asha wants to buy a mobile phone.

She finds an online shop that has a sale that offers 20% of all mobile phones.

On Black Friday, the online shop reduces all sale prices on mobile phones by a further 30%.

Asha buys a mobile phone on Black Friday.

Work out the final percentage reduction that Asha receives on the price of the mobile phone.

..................................%

(Total for Question 24 is 4 marks)

Turn to page 155 for complete worked solutions to the questions on this page.

ALGEBRA

 Revision Guide
Page 39

Hint

If two lines have different gradients then they are **not parallel**. This means that they must intersect.

Hint

To find the gradient of line A rearrange it into the form $y = mx + x$. The value of m is the gradient.

Watch out!

Remember the gradient doesn't have to be a whole number.

Hint

To find the gradient of the second line draw a sketch showing a line through the two points. Draw a triangle and use it to find the gradient:

25 A and B are straight lines.
Line A has the equation $3y = 2x + 8$
Line B goes through the points $(-1, 2)$ and $(2, 8)$

Do lines A and B intersect?
You must show your working

Scan this QR code for a video of this question being solved!

(Total for Question 25 is 3 marks)

TOTAL FOR PAPER IS 80 MARKS

Turn to page 155 for complete worked solutions to the questions on this page.

Paper 2: Calculator
Time allowed: 1 hour 30 minutes

1   Simplify $3 \times c \times d$

....
(Total for Question 1 is 1 mark)

2   Simplify $3x + 7y + 2x - y$

....
(Total for Question 2 is 2 marks)

3   Expand $t(3t^2 + 4)$

....
(Total for Question 3 is 2 marks)

4   Write 178% as a decimal.

....
(Total for Question 4 is 1 mark)

Turn to page 156 for complete worked solutions to the questions on this page.

 ALGEBRA

 Revision Guide
Page 23

Hint

You just need to write this expression without multiplication signs.

Revision Guide
Page 22

Hint

Group the x terms and the y terms. Remember the sign (+ or −) goes with the term after it.

 Revision Guide
Page 28

Hint

Multiply the term outside the brackets by **both** terms inside the brackets.

Hint

$t \times 3t^2 = 3t^3$

 RATIO & PROPORTION

 Revision Guide
Page 56

Hint

Divide by 100 to convert from a percentage to a decimal.

Revision Guide
Pages 1, 5

Hint

For part **(a)**, Sameena needs to buy a **whole number** of cups of coffee. You could:

- divide £10 by £1.40 then round **down** to the next whole number
- work out ☐ × £1.40 for some different values. Find the largest number of cups of coffee that costs less than £10

Hint

Divide by 2 to find half of something.

Watch out!

You might not need to use all of the information given in a question. Read carefully to work out which values to use.

---

5   Here is the menu in Sam's Cafe.

> **Sam's Cafe**
>
> | | |
> |---|---|
> | cup of tea | £1.20 |
> | cup of coffee | £1.40 |
> | breakfast: sausage, eggs, bacon | £4.10 |
> | special: sausage, eggs, bacon and toast | £4.50 |

Sameena buys some cups of coffee.
She only has £10

(a) Work out the greatest number of cups of coffee she can buy.

.... cups

(2)

A child's meal costs half of the cost of the special.

(b) Work out the cost of a child's meal.

£ ....

(1)

(Total for Question 5 is 3 marks)

Turn to page 156 for complete worked solutions to the questions on this page.

6 Jack makes a fair 6-sided spinner for a game.

 PROBABILITY & STATISTICS

Revision Guide
Page 128

Jack will spin the spinner once.
The spinner will land on one of the numbers.

(a) Draw a circle around the word that best describes the
probability of this event.

The spinner will land on 3

impossible	unlikely	evens	likely	certain

(1)

Jack makes a different fair 6-sided spinner.
The spinner only has the numbers 1, 2 and 3 on it.

The probability that the spinner will land on 1 is $\frac{1}{2}$

The probability that the spinner will land on 2 is greater than the
probability that the spinner will land on 3

(b) Write the numbers on the spinner.

(2)
(Total for Question 6 is 3 marks)

Hint

1 out of 6 segments
has the number 3 on it.
Describe a one-in-six
chance in words.

LEARN IT!

Hint

If P(1) = $\frac{1}{2}$ then exactly
half of the segments
on the spinner must be
labelled 1

Problem solved!

Once you have labelled
your spinner, reread
the question. **Check**
that your answer
matches **all** the
information given.

Turn to page 156 for complete worked solutions to the questions on this page.

Revision Guide
Page 25

Investigate how your
calculator interprets
brackets and order of
operations. Try entering
these calculations:

$$4 \times 2^3$$

$$(4 \times 2)^3$$

 ALGEBRA

Revision Guide
Page 50

Hint

You need to rearrange
the formula so that c is
on its own on one side.

Watch out!

Always apply the
same operation to
both sides of the
formula. Write down the
operation you are using
at each stage.

 Explore

When $b = 2$ and
$c = 3$ then
$a = 2 + 5 \times 3 = 17$
Substitute these values
into your rearranged
formula. Do they still
work?

---

7 Work out the value of $4x^3$ when $x = 2$

....

(Total for Question 7 is 1 mark)

---

8 Make c the subject of the formula $a = b + 5c$

....

(Total for Question 8 is 2 marks)

Turn to page 156 for complete worked solutions to the questions on this page.

9   Solve $4m + 6 = 15$

 ALGEBRA

 Revision Guide
Page 30

Hint

You need to do **two steps** to get m on its own. The first step is to subtract 6 from both sides of the equation.

Hint

You can check your answer by substituting it into $4m + 6$. The answer should be 15

Explore

This equation is like this balance:

$m = $ ....
(Total for Question 9 is 2 marks)

Turn to page 157 for complete worked solutions to the questions on this page.

RATIO & PROPORTION

 Revision Guide Page 61

Problem solved!

You are given Sandeep's answer and you need to check it. The easiest way to do this is to work out the weight of 460 screws, then add the weight of the empty box. Compare your answer with 1.21 kg and write a short conclusion.

Hint

1.21 kg = 1.21 × 1000
= 1210 grams

 ### Explore

When you have hundreds of items, small differences can have a big effect. How much heavier would the box be if each screw weighed 2.6 grams?

---

10 A box containing screws weighs 1.21 kilograms.
Each screw weighs 2.5 grams.
When empty, the box weighs 60 grams.

Sandeep says: "The number of screws in the box is 460."
Is Sandeep correct? You must show your working.

(Total for Question 10 is 4 marks)

Turn to page 157 for complete worked solutions to the questions on this page.

11

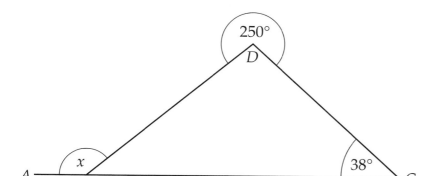

ABC is a straight line.
Angle *BCD* = 38°
The reflex angle *BDC* = 250°
Work out the size of the angle marked *x*.
Give reasons for your answer.

GEOMETRY &
MEASURES

Revision Guide
Pages 73, 74

Hint

You can use these
angle facts:
• angles around a point
  add up to 360°
• angles in a triangle
  add up to 180°
• angles on a straight
  line add up to 180°

Watch out!

You need to write down
reasons for **each step**
of your working, using
correct mathematical
language.

Problem solved!

Plan your strategy
before you start. Look
at the diagram and
work out which angles
you can work out from
the information given.

x = ... °

(Total for Question 11 is 4 marks)

Turn to page 157 for complete worked solutions to the questions on this page.

NUMBER

 RATIO & PROPORTION

 Revision Guide
Pages 4, 5, 61

LEARN IT!

1 m = 100 cm

Hint

For part **(b)**, you are interested in the **width** of each shelf, not the height.

Problem solved!

Solutions to some word problems must be **whole numbers**. Amy can't put a fraction of a DVD on the shelf, so round down to the nearest whole number.

 Explore

Amy could fit 45 DVDs on a single shelf that was twice as wide. (640 ÷ 14 = 45.71...) Explain why this is different from the answer to part **(b)**.

---

12   Amy is making a shelf unit for her DVDs.

She needs:

   3 pieces of wood of length 32 cm
and 2 pieces of wood of length 45 cm.

Amy has a piece of wood of length 2 metres.
She cuts the 5 pieces of wood she needs from the 2 metre length of wood.

(a) What length of wood does Amy have left from the 2 metre length?

....
(3)

The diagram shows the shelf unit.

Amy will put DVDs on the 2 shelves, as shown in the diagram. Each DVD has a width of 14 mm.

(b) What is the greatest number of DVDs Amy can put on the 2 shelves?

.... DVDs
(3)
(Total for Question 12 is 6 marks)

Turn to page 157 for complete worked solutions to the questions on this page.

13   Alan, Ben and Clara are playing a card game.

Alan has p cards.
Ben has twice as many cards as Alan.
Clara has 3 cards fewer than Ben.

They have a total of 17 cards.

Work out how many cards each person has.

Alan: .... cards

Ben: .... cards

Clara: .... cards

(Total for Question 13 is 4 marks)

Turn to page 158 for complete worked solutions to the questions on this page.

√xy² **ALGEBRA**

Revision Guide
Pages 22, 51

Hint

Write expressions for the number of cards Ben and Clara each have, in terms of p.

Hint

Add together your expressions then simplify the expression.

Problem solved!

If a question gives you a letter to represent an unknown value, you should try and use algebra to solve the problem. This will be quicker than trying different numbers.

Watch out!

Check by adding together your three numbers. The total should be 17

NUMBER

 Revision Guide
Page 13

Problem solved!

Here are two possible strategies:
1. Work out the number of blue and red counters, then subtract this from 200
2. Work out $1 - \left(\frac{1}{4} + \frac{2}{5}\right)$, then find this fraction of 200

Hint

To find $\frac{2}{5}$ of 200 work out $200 \times \frac{2}{5}$. You can enter fractions on your calculator using the ▣ key.

Explore

$\frac{2}{5}$ of 200 and $\frac{1}{4}$ of 200 are both whole numbers. But $\frac{1}{3}$ of $200 = 66.666\ldots$ is not a whole number. Any fraction whose denominator is a **factor** of 200 will give a whole number answer. Find all the possible denominators that could give a whole number of a given colour.

14   There are 200 counters in a bag.
The counters are blue or red or yellow.

$\frac{1}{4}$ of the counters are blue.

$\frac{2}{5}$ of the counters are red.

Work out the number of yellow counters in the bag.

....

(Total for Question 14 is 4 marks)

Turn to page 158 for complete worked solutions to the questions on this page.

15 Here is the number of goals scored by a football team in each of its first 10 games.

     3   1   4   2   0   1   1   1   3   2

(a) Write down the mode.

....
(1)

(b) Work out the mean number of goals for the first 10 games.

....
(2)

In the 11th game the team scored 4 goals.
In the 12th game the team scored 2 goals.

(c) Will the mean number of goals for the 12 games be greater than or less than the mean number of goals for the first 10 games? You must explain your answer.

....

....

....
(2)

(Total for Question 15 is 5 marks)

Turn to page 158 for complete worked solutions to the questions on this page.

 PROBABILITY & STATISTICS

Revision Guide
Page 120

Watch out!

For the mode, make sure you write down the most common data value, not the number of times it occurs.

LEARN IT!

To find the mean, add up all the data values, then divide by the number of data values.

Hint

The **mode** is always one of the data values. So here, the mode must be a **whole number**. The mean does not have to be one of the data values, so it can be a decimal.

Problem solved!

For part **(c)** you don't actually have to calculate the new mean. Compare the two new data values with the mean for the first 10 games, then write a short conclusion.

RATIO & PROPORTION

Revision Guide
Pages 1, 60, 61

Problem solved!

Start by working out how much of each ingredient is needed to make 1 jam roll. You need to divide 425 g in the ratio 8 : 4 : 5

Hint

Multiply the weights in grams needed for 1 jam roll by 200 to find the amounts of each ingredient needed.

Watch out!

Remember to convert from grams to kg by dividing by 1000

Watch out!

Be careful with £ and pence. You should convert the cost of flour into £ before calculating.

Hint

Remember to compare your final amount with £90 and write a conclusion.

---

16 A baker makes jam rolls.

The baker uses flour, butter and jam in the ratio 8 : 4 : 5 to make jam rolls.

The table shows the cost per kilogram of some of these ingredients.

Cost per kilogram	
Flour	40p
Butter	£2.50
Jam	£1.00

The total weight of the flour, butter and jam for each jam roll is 425 g.

The baker wants to make 200 jam rolls. He has £90 to spend on the ingredients.

Does he have enough money?
You must show your working.

(Total for Question 16 is 5 marks)

Turn to page 158 for complete worked solutions to the questions on this page.

17 There are 130 adults at a language school.
Each adult studies either French or Spanish or German.

96 of the adults are women.
12 of the women study French.
73 of the adults study Spanish.
55 of the women study Spanish.
9 of the men study German.

(a) Complete the two-way table.

	French	Spanish	German	Total
Men				
Women				
Total				

(3)

(b) One adult is chosen at random.
Work out the probability that they are a man who studies Spanish.

....
(2)

Scan this QR code for a video of this question being solved!

(Total for Question 17 is 5 marks)

PROBABILITY & STATISTICS

Revision Guide Page 115

Hint

There are 130 adults in total, so write 130 in the bottom right-hand corner.

Hint

Enter each piece of information from the list. It's a good idea to cross them off as you go.

Hint

The entries in each row or column add up to the total for that row or column. Use addition and subtraction to find any missing entries.

Watch out!

Check that the row totals add up to 130, and that the column totals add up to 130

Turn to page 159 for complete worked solutions to the questions on this page.

Revision Guide
Page 68

Problem solved!

The prices are given in £ so work out how much Simon has in total in £. Then compare this amount with the prices of the items he wants to buy and write a short conclusion.

Hint

You can round answers in pounds to 2 decimal places.

Hint

Use the exchange rate to convert:

× 21.62

£1 = 21.62 rand

÷ 21.62

---

18 Simon has £200 and 3700 rand.

He goes to a shop where he can spend both pounds and rand.

He wants to buy:

  a computer costing £360

or

  a watch costing £400

or

  a camera costing £375

The conversion rate is £1 = 21.62 rand.

Which of these items can Simon afford to buy?
You must show clearly how you get your answer.

(Total for Question 18 is 3 marks)

Turn to page 159 for complete worked solutions to the questions on this page.

19 A bank pays compound interest of 9.25% per annum.
Ravina invests £8600 for 3 years.

(a) Calculate the interest earned after 3 years.

£ ....

(3)

(b) Show that the interest gained after 3 years is 30.4% of her original investment.

(2)

(Total for Question 19 is 5 marks)

% RATIO & PROPORTION

Revision Guide Page 63

Hint

To find the multiplier for a percentage increase, add the increase to 100 then divide by 100:
$$\frac{100 + 9.25}{100} = 1.0925$$

Watch out!

You need to find the **interest**, not the total amount in Ravina's account. Subtract £8600 from the total amount to find the interest earned.

Hint

Divide the interest by the original investment.

LEARN IT!

Use this formula to find the total amount after n years:
starting amount
$\times (\text{multiplier})^n$

Turn to page 159 for complete worked solutions to the questions on this page.

NUMBER

 RATIO & PROPORTION

 Revision Guide
Pages 17, 59, 61

Hint

You need to write quantities in the same units before comparing them. Convert 7.8×10^8 km into metres by multiplying by 1000

Hint

You can enter numbers in standard form on your calculator using the $\boxed{\times 10^x}$ key.

LEARN IT!

Your calculator should give you the answer in standard form. Check that:

- the first part is a number ≥ 1 and < 10
- the second part is a power of 10

Problem solved!

Write the ratio in the form $8 : \square$, then divide both sides by 8 to get an equivalent ratio in the form $1 : n$

20 Rob is making a scale model of the Solar System on the school field. He wants the distance from the Sun to Jupiter to be 8 metres on his scale model.

The real distance from the Sun to Jupiter is 7.8×10^8 kilometres.

Find the scale of the model.
Give your answer in the form $1 : n$, where n is written in standard form.

Scan this QR code for a video of this question being solved!

1 : ....

(Total for Question 20 is 3 marks)

Turn to page 159 for complete worked solutions to the questions on this page.

21 A steel rod has a density of 7.6 g per cm³.
The rod has a mass of 200 g.

Work out the volume of the rod.
Give your answer correct to 3 significant figures.

steel rod

 **RATIO &
PROPORTION**

 Revision Guide
Page 65

Hint

Draw the formula
triangle for density at
the top of your working:

$$\frac{M}{D \mid V}$$

Hint

Write down at least
4 d.p. from your
calculator display
before rounding to
3 significant figures.

Explore

The units of density
give you a clue about
how to work it out.
The units are grams
per cm³ or g/cm³. To
find density you divide
mass (g) by volume
(cm³). Investigate the
units used for speed
and pressure. Use
these to draw the
formula triangles for
calculating speed and
pressure.

....
(Total for Question 21 is 3 marks)

Turn to page 160 for complete worked solutions to the questions on this page.

GEOMETRY &
MEASURES

Revision Guide
Page 74

Watch out!

The diagram is not accurately drawn, so you have to use angle facts to determine whether the lines are parallel.

Watch out!

You don't know that the lines are parallel, so you can't use angle facts about parallel lines in your working.

Problem solved!

If you can show that two **corresponding angles** are equal then the lines are parallel:

Hint

Give reasons for **every step** of your working.

22 The diagram shows a side view of a kitchen step ladder.

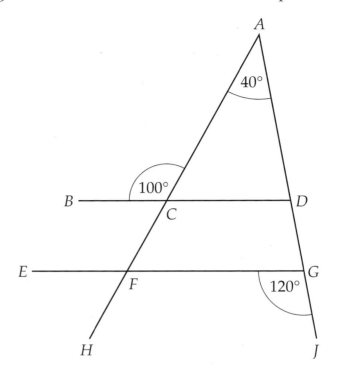

Brian says the straight lines *BCD* and *EFG* are parallel.

Is Brian correct?
You must show all your working.
Give reasons for your answer.

....

....

....

....

....

....

....

....

(Total for Question 22 is 3 marks)

Turn to page 160 for complete worked solutions to the questions on this page.

23 *PQR* is the side of a vertical building.

AB is a ramp.
AP is horizontal ground.
BQ is a horizontal path.

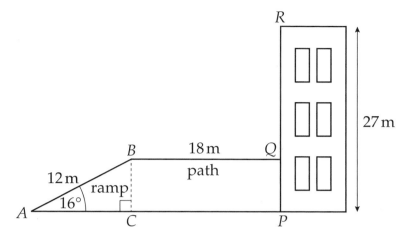

The building has a height of 27 m.
The ramp *AB* is at an angle of 16° to the horizontal ground.
The ramp has a length of 12 m. The path has a length of 18 m.

(a) Work out the height of the ramp.
Give your answer correct to 3 significant figures.

.....................................m
(2)

(b) Show that the angle of elevation of the top of the building, *R*,
from the top of the ramp, *B*, is 52.8° correct to 3 significant figures.

(3)
(Total for Question 23 is 5 marks)

GEOMETRY & MEASURES

 Revision Guide
Pages 92, 93

LEARN IT!

Remember
S^O_H C^A_H T^O_A:

$\sin x = \dfrac{opp}{hyp}$

$\cos x = \dfrac{adj}{hyp}$

$\tan x = \dfrac{opp}{adj}$

Hint

For part **(a)** you know
hyp and want the **opp**
so use sin.

Hint

You need to use the
$\boxed{\tan^{-1}}$ function on your
calculator to find the
angle in part **(b)**.

Watch out!

The height of the
triangle for part **(b)**
is the height of the
building **minus** your
answer to part **(a)**.

Hint

Write down at least
4 decimal places from
your calculator display
before rounding your
answer.

Turn to page 160 for complete worked solutions to the questions on this page.

Revision Guide
Page 44

LEARN IT!

The quadratic graph with equation $y = (x - a)(x - b)$ crosses the x-axis at $(a, 0)$ and $(b, 0)$. The graph is **symmetrical** so the minimum point is halfway between these points.

Watch out!

You need to find the x-coordinate **and the y-coordinate** of the minimum point.

Problem solved!

Find the x-coordinate of the minimum point then substitute this into the equation to find the y-coordinate.

Hint

Check that your answer makes sense. The x-coordinate will be positive and the y-coordinate will be negative.

24 Here is a sketch of the curve with equation $y = (x - 2)(x - 8)$

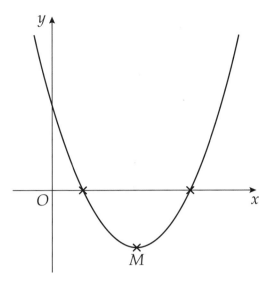

Work out the coordinates of the minimum point, M, of the curve.

Scan this QR code for a video of this question being solved!

(....................., ...)

(Total for Question 24 is 4 marks)

TOTAL FOR PAPER IS 80 MARKS

Turn to page 160 for complete worked solutions to the questions on this page.

Paper 3: Calculator
Time allowed: 1 hour 30 minutes

1   Write down 23 507 to the nearest thousand.

....
(Total for Question 1 is 1 mark)

2   (a) Simplify $3m + 7m - 2m$

....
(1)

(b) Simplify $a^3 + a^3$

....
(1)
(Total for Question 2 is 2 marks)

NUMBER

Revision Guide
Page 3

Hint

To round to the nearest thousand look at the digit in the hundreds place. If it is 5 or more round up. If it is less than 5 round down.

ALGEBRA

Revision Guide
Page 22

Hint

How many lots of m are there in total?

Hint

a^3 is the same as '1 lot of a^3'

Turn to page 161 for complete worked solutions to the questions on this page.

NUMBER

 Revision Guide
Page 13

Hint

You can use your calculator for part **(a)**. Enter each fraction and press $=$ to get the fraction in lowest terms.

It's easiest to compare fractions when they have the **same denominator**. In part **(b)**, try writing both fractions as equivalent fractions with denominator 60

Explore

You could also use your calculator for part **(b)**. Write both fractions as decimals. Choose a decimal between these two numbers, then write it as a fraction.

3 Here are five fractions.

$$\frac{5}{20} \qquad \frac{9}{36} \qquad \frac{25}{100} \qquad \frac{12}{52} \qquad \frac{17}{68}$$

(a) Find which one of these is **not** equal to $\frac{1}{4}$

....
(1)

(b) Find a fraction between $\frac{1}{6}$ and $\frac{1}{5}$

....
(2)
(Total for Question 3 is 3 marks)

Turn to page 161 for complete worked solutions to the questions on this page.

4 Here is a list of eight numbers

4   5   25   29   30   33   39   40

From the list, write down

(a) a factor of 20

....

(1)

(b) a multiple of 10

....

(1)

(c) a prime number that is greater than 15

....

(1)

(Total for Question 4 is 3 marks)

NUMBER

Revision Guide
Page 11

You need to be able to
recognise the prime
numbers less than 50

Hint

The **multiples** of a
number are the numbers
in its times table.

Explore

Every number is a
multiple of itself and
every number is a
factor of itself.

PROBABILITY & STATISTICS

Revision Guide
Page 119

Hint

For part **(a)** you can describe the type of correlation, or you can say what happens when the length of a dolphin increases.

Hint

For part **(b)** you need to draw a **line of best fit** on the scatter graph. Slide a transparent ruler across the scatter graph. Aim to have the same number of points on each side of your line.

Hint

Now read up from 2.3 m on the horizontal axis to your line of best fit, then across to the vertical axis.

Problem solved!

For part **(d)** you can say that the estimate is reliable or unreliable, as long as you **justify** your answer.

5 A scientist recorded the lengths and the weights of 8 dolphins. The scatter graph shows information about these dolphins.

(a) Describe the relationship between the length and the weight of these dolphins.

....

(1)

A dolphin has a length of 2.54 metres and a weight of 132 kg.

(b) Show this information on the scatter graph.

(1)

A dolphin has a length of 2.3 metres.

(c) Estimate the weight of this dolphin.

.... kg

(2)

(d) Comment on the reliability of the answer in part (c).

....

....

(1)

(Total for Question 5 is 5 marks)

Turn to page 161 for complete worked solutions to the questions on this page.

6   Solve $2x + 3 = 10$

 √xy² ALGEBRA

Revision Guide
Page 30

Hint

To solve an equation
you need to get the
letter on its own on
one side. Use inverse
operations. Subtract 3
from both sides, then
divide both sides by 2

Watch out!

The solution to an
equation does not have
to be a whole number.

Explore

If you substitute your
answer into $2x + 3$
you should get the
answer 10

$x = $ ....
(Total for Question 6 is 2 marks)

Revision Guide
Page 1

LEARN IT!

Profit means the total Simon sells his items for must be more than the amount he bought them for. **Loss** means the opposite – he spent more money than he got back.

Problem solved!

You only need to show working to explain whether Simon makes a profit or a loss. You don't need to work out the amount of the profit or loss.

Hint

Make sure you compare the total Simon spent with £45.75 before writing a short conclusion.

---

7   Simon goes to a car boot sale.

He buys:

     4 cups and saucers for a total of £15.95
     4 plates at £1.35 each
     6 egg cups for a total of £7.20.

Simon sells all the items he buys for a total of £45.75.

Does he make a profit or a loss?
You must show all your working.

 Scan this QR code for a video of this question being solved!

(Total for Question 7 is 4 marks)

Turn to page 162 for complete worked solutions to the questions on this page.

8   Expand $3(2 + t)$

....

(Total for Question 8 is 1 mark)

9   Expand $3x(2x + 5)$

....

(Total for Question 9 is 2 marks)

√xy²   ALGEBRA

Revision Guide
Page 28

Hint

Multiply the number outside the brackets by **every term** inside the brackets.

√xy²   ALGEBRA

Revision Guide
Pages 23, 28

Watch out!

Be careful:
$3x \times 2x = 3 \times 2 \times x \times x$

Explore

If $x = 2$, then
$3x(2x + 5) = 6 \times 9$
$= 54$
Substitute $x = 2$ into your answer and check that the answer is 54

Turn to page 162 for complete worked solutions to the questions on this page.

115

Revision Guide
Page 55

LEARN IT!

Simple interest means that the starting amount stays the **same** each year.

Hint

To find 4% of £300 work out $\frac{4}{100}$ × £300. You can use the ▦ key on your calculator to enter a fraction.

Watch out!

Read percentages questions carefully. Are you being asked for the amount of interest or VAT, or the total amount after the percentage increase?

---

10 Jeremy invests £300 for two years at 4% simple interest each year.

(a) Work out the amount of interest he will get at the end of two years.

£ ....

(3)

Jeremy buys a TV.
He pays £450 plus 20% VAT.

(b) Work out the VAT.

£ ....

(2)

(Total for Question 10 is 5 marks)

Turn to page 162 for complete worked solutions to the questions on this page.

11

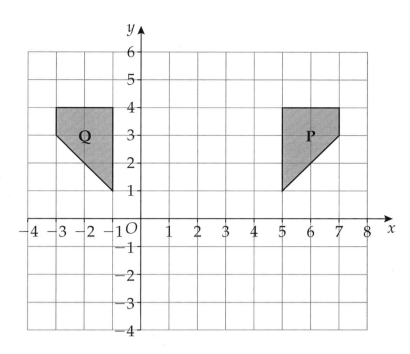

(a) Describe fully the single transformation which maps shape **P** onto shape **Q**.

(2)

(b) Reflect the shape **Q** in the line $y = x$
Label the new shape **R**.

(2)

Scan this QR code for a video of this question being solved!

(Total for Question 11 is 4 marks)

RATIO & PROPORTION

Revision Guide
Page 67

Hint

If you need to convert between metric units (like km) and imperial units (like miles) in your exam, you will be given the conversion with the question.

Hint

To convert km to miles you divide by 8 then multiply by 5

Watch out!

Check that your answer makes sense. The number of miles must be **less** than the number of km.

Explore

A surveyor needs to drive along every road on this map. Plan his route so he travels the shortest distance possible. Can you find a route that is less than 2700 km? (Hint: he will need to drive along at least one road more than once.)

---

12 The map shows the distances, in kilometres, between some towns and cities in France.

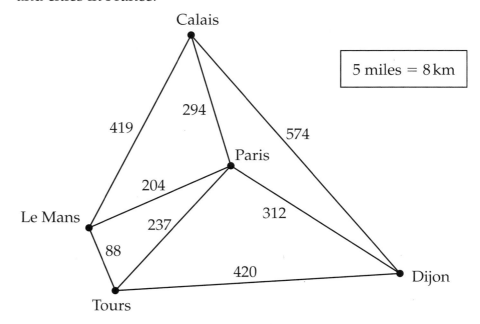

5 miles = 8 km

Fiona is on holiday in France.
She drives from Calais to Paris.
She then drives from Paris to Dijon.

Work out the total distance she travels in miles.

.... miles

(Total for Question 12 is 3 marks)

Turn to page 163 for complete worked solutions to the questions on this page.

13 (a) Work out $\dfrac{4.6 + 3.85}{3.2^2 - 6.51}$

Write down all the numbers on your calculator display.

....
(2)

(b) Write down your answer correct to 3 significant figures.

....
(1)

(Total for Question 13 is 3 marks)

Turn to page 163 for complete worked solutions to the questions on this page.

 NUMBER

Revision Guide
Page 16

Hint

Work out what the top and bottom of the fraction come to, and write these down before dividing.

Watch out!

Part **(a)** tells you to write down **all** the numbers on your calculator display, so don't round your answer.

Explore

Confirm that your calculator works out indices (powers) before subtraction. These should give the same answer:

$$3.2^2 - 6.51$$

$$(3.2)^2 - 6.51$$

GEOMETRY &
MEASURES

 Revision Guide
Pages 98, 102

Hint

Measure lengths
accurate to the nearest
mm.

Hint

The scale is 4 cm = 1 km.
Measure the distance
on the drawing in cm,
then divide by 4 to get
the real-life distance in
km.

Hint

In part **(b)** you need
to use a protractor to
measure the bearing of
A from B. Draw a line
on this bearing, then
measure 6 cm along the
line with a ruler.

 LEARN IT!

Bearings are always
measured **clockwise**
from North.

Explore

The bearing of A from
B is 038°. This means
that the bearing of B
from A is
38° + 180° = 218°.
Measure it on your
drawing to check.

---

14 The diagram shows the positions of two villages, Beckhampton (*B*)
and West Kennett (*W*). The diagram is drawn accurately.

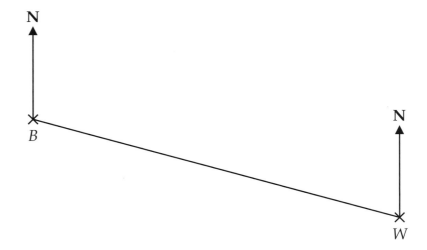

Scale: 4 cm represents 1 km.

(a) Work out the real distance, in kilometres, of Beckhampton from
West Kennett.

.... km

(2)

The village Avebury (*A*) is on a bearing of 038° from Beckhampton.

On the diagram, *A* is 6 cm from *B*.

(b) On the diagram, mark *A* with a cross (×).
Label the cross *A*.

(2)

(Total for Question 14 is 4 marks)

Turn to page 163 for complete worked solutions to the questions on this page.

15 The speed, v, of a car is 73 miles per hour, correct to the nearest whole number.

Write down the error interval for the speed of the car.

Turn to page 164 for complete worked solutions to the questions on this page.

 $\leq v <$ ....

(Total for Question 15 is 2 marks)

Revision Guide
Pages 3, 32

Hint

The speed is rounded to the nearest whole number. The actual value could be up to **half a unit** higher or lower.

Explore

You use $\leq$ (less than or equal to) for the lower bound, and $<$ (less than) for the upper bound.

121

GEOMETRY & MEASURES

Revision Guide
Page 101

Hint

You can find the centre of the rectangle by drawing the **diagonals**. The point where they intersect is the centre.

Hint

Set your compasses to 2 cm and draw a circle with its centre at the centre of the rectangle.

Hint

Measure 2 cm from the side *BC* along the top **and** the bottom, then join these points with a straight line.

Watch out!

Read the last part of the question carefully to work out which areas to shade.

---

16 Here is an accurate scale diagram of a car park in the shape of a rectangle.

The scale is 1 cm to 10 m.

Cars must **not** be parked:

　　within 20 m of the centre of the rectangle

or

　　within 20 m of the side *BC*.

On the diagram, show accurately by shading, the regions where cars must not be parked.

Scan this QR code for a video of this question being solved!

(Total for Question 16 is 4 marks)

　　Turn to page 164 for complete worked solutions to the questions on this page.

17 Factorise $x^2 + 7x$

....

(Total for Question 17 is 1 mark)

Revision Guide
Page 29

Hint

Check your answer by expanding the brackets – you should get the original expression.

Hint

Write x outside the brackets for this expression.

18 Factorise $y^2 - 10y + 16$

....

(Total for Question 18 is 2 marks)

Revision Guide
Page 46

Hint

This is a **quadratic** expression. You need to find two numbers that add up to -10 and multiply to give 16

Hint

The factorised expression will be in the form $(y - \square)(y - \square)$

Turn to page 164 for complete worked solutions to the questions on this page.

NUMBER

 Revision Guide
Page 17

LEARN IT!

For a number in standard form:
- the first part is a number ≥1 and <10
- the second part is a power of 10

Hint

Count decimal places to convert between ordinary numbers and standard form.

Problem solved!

If you're not sure what calculation to do for part **(c)**, try simpler numbers first:

A box of lemons weighs 2.4 kg. Each lemon weighs 0.1 kg. How many lemons are in the box?

Hint

Use brackets when entering standard form numbers into your calculator.

---

19 The distance of the Earth from Mars is 5.5×10^7 kilometres.

(a) Write 5.5×10^7 as an ordinary number.

....

(1)

The diameter of Jupiter is 143 000 kilometres.

(b) Write 143 000 in standard form.

....

(1)

One light year is the distance travelled by light in one year.

One astronomical unit (au) is the average distance from the Sun to the Earth.

One light year = 9.461×10^{12} km
One astronomical unit = 1.496×10^8 km

(c) How many astronomical units are there in a light year?

Give your answer in standard form correct to 3 significant figures.

.... au

(2)

(Total for Question 19 is 4 marks)

Turn to page 164 for complete worked solutions to the questions on this page.

20 Greg sells car insurance and home insurance.
The table shows the cost of these insurances.

Insurance	Car insurance	Home insurance
Cost	£200	£350

Each month Greg earns:

£530 basic pay plus

5% commission of the cost of all the car insurance he sells

and 10% commission of the cost of all the home insurance he sells.

In May, Greg sold:

6 car insurances

and 4 home insurances.

Work out the total amount of money Greg earned in May.

£ ....

(Total for Question 20 is 4 marks)

Turn to page 165 for complete worked solutions to the questions on this page.

NUMBER

RATIO & PROPORTION

 Revision Guide
Pages 1, 55

Hint

Here are three possible calculations to find 5% of 200:

- $\frac{5}{100} \times 200$
- 200×0.05
- $200 \div 20$

Hint

You could also use a multiplier to find this percentage. 10% of 350 is the same as 0.1×350

Problem solved!

The safest strategy here is to find the amount of commission Greg earns on each insurance. Then add up

- his basic pay
- 6 lots of his car insurance commission
- 4 lots of his home insurance commission.

Watch out!

Write out the calculations that you use, even if you are using a calculator.

RATIO & PROPORTION

 Revision Guide
Page 62

Watch out!

This is a **reverse percentages** question. You are given the amount **after** the decrease, and you need to find the **original amount**.

Hint

Here are two possible strategies:

1. Find the multiplier for a 70% decrease, then **divide** 90 by the multiplier.

2. Divide 90 by 30 to find 1%, then multiply by 100 to find 100%.

Hint

70% is more than half off. Check that £90 is less than half of your answer.

21 In a sale the price of paving slabs is reduced by 70%.
Josie buys some paving slabs at the sale price of £90.

What was the original price of the paving slabs?

 Scan this QR code for a video of this question being solved!

£ ....

(2)

(Total for Question 21 is 2 marks)

Turn to page 165 for complete worked solutions to the questions on this page.

22 Use a ruler and compasses to construct the bisector of this angle.
You must show all your construction lines.

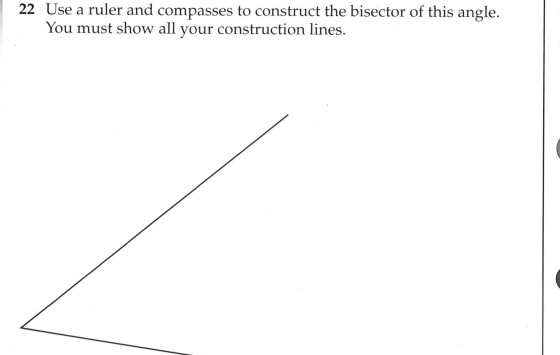

(Total for Question 22 is 2 marks)

 GEOMETRY & MEASURES

Revision Guide
Page 100

Watch out!

Always leave all your **construction marks** on your diagram so you can show your method.

Hint

Use a ruler and a sharp pencil.

Hint

You can leave your compasses set to the same distance throughout this construction.

 Explore

You can exactly **bisect** an angle (divide it in two) using only a straight edge and compasses. However, it is impossible to **trisect** an angle (divide it in three) in this way.

Turn to page 165 for complete worked solutions to the questions on this page.

PROBABILITY
& STATISTICS

Revision Guide
Page 129

LEARN IT!

The probability of all
the different outcomes
of an event add up to 1

Hint

For part **(a)** add up all
the probabilities, then
subtract the result
from 1

LEARN IT!

Expected number of
outcomes =
Number of trials ×
probability

Watch out!

Check that your
answer makes sense.
It must be more than
0 and less than 40

23 A box contains some coloured cards.
Each card is red or blue or yellow or green.
The table shows the probability of taking a red card or a blue card
or a yellow card.

Card	Probability
Red	0.3
Blue	0.35
Yellow	0.15
Green	

George takes, at random, a card from the box.

(a) Work out the probability that George takes a green card.

....

(2)

George replaces his card in the box.
Anish takes a card from the box and then replaces the card.
Anish does this 40 times.

(b) Work out an estimate for the number of times Anish takes a
yellow card.

....

(2)
(Total for Question 23 is 4 marks)

Turn to page 165 for complete worked solutions to the questions on this page.

24 The diagram shows a right-angled triangle and a rectangle.

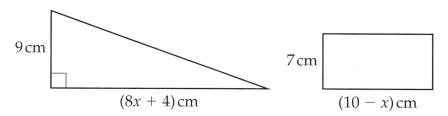

9 cm

(8x + 4) cm

7 cm

(10 − x) cm

The area of the triangle is twice the area of the rectangle.

Find the area of the rectangle.
Show clear algebraic working.

$\sqrt{xy^2}$ **ALGEBRA**

 Revision Guide
Page 51

LEARN IT!

Area of triangle
= $\frac{1}{2}$ × base × height

Problem solved!

You need to use algebra to solve this problem. Find expressions for the area of each shape **in terms of x**. Then set the area of the triangle equal to twice the area of the rectangle. This gives you an equation that you can solve to find x.

Watch out!

Read the question carefully. After you find x you need to work out the **area of the rectangle**.

Watch out!

Solutions to equations don't have to be whole numbers.

..................................cm²
(Total for Question 24 is 5 marks)

Turn to page 166 for complete worked solutions to the questions on this page.

PROBABILITY & STATISTICS

Revision Guide
Page 122

Hint

The modal class interval is the class interval with the highest frequency. Make sure you write down the class interval and **not** the frequency.

Hint

To find the mean, add two columns to the table. One for 'midpoint' and one for 'frequency × midpoint'.

Problem solved!

For part **(c)** think about whether the new data value will **increase** or **decrease** the mean, and write a conclusion.

Explore

Your answer to part **(b)** will be an estimate because you don't know the exact data values. You are assuming that each data value is in the middle of its class interval.

25 The table shows information about the amount of money, in dollars, spent in a shop in one day by 80 people.

Money spent (x dollars)	Frequency
$0 < x \leqslant 20$	24
$20 < x \leqslant 40$	20
$40 < x \leqslant 60$	9
$60 < x \leqslant 80$	12
$80 < x \leqslant 100$	15

(a) Write down the modal class interval.

....
(1)

(b) Work out an estimate for the mean amount of money spent in that shop that day.

.... dollars
(3)

One more person spent 84 dollars.

(c) How will this affect the mean?

You must give a reason.

(1)
(Total for Question 25 is 5 marks)

Turn to page 166 for complete worked solutions to the questions on this page.

26 The diagram shows a parallelogram, *PQRS*.

M is the midpoint of *PS*.

$\overrightarrow{PM} = \mathbf{a}$ $\overrightarrow{PQ} = \mathbf{b}$

Find, in terms of **a** and/or **b**:

(a) $\overrightarrow{PS}$

....
(1)

(b) $\overrightarrow{PR}$

....
(1)

(c) $\overrightarrow{MQ}$

....
(1)

(Total for Question 26 is 3 marks)

TOTAL FOR PAPER IS 80 MARKS

GEOMETRY & MEASURES

Revision Guide Page 112

Hint

M is the midpoint of *PS*, so the distance from *P* to *S* is **twice** the distance from *P* to *M*. This means that $\overrightarrow{PS} = 2 \times \overrightarrow{PM}$

Hint

For part **(c)**, trace a path from *M* to *Q*. If you go **backwards** along a vector you have to **subtract** that vector.

Hint

Don't try and write **a** and **b** in bold in your answer! Just use normal neat letters.

Turn to page 166 for complete worked solutions to the questions on this page.

Paper 1: Non-calculator
Time allowed: 1 hour 30 minutes

1 Work out -3×-9

27 ✓
(Total for Question 1 is 1 mark)

2 (a) Work out $9 + 6 \div 2$
$9 + 3 = 12$

12 ✓
(1)

(b) Work out $(15 + 5) \times (5 - 3)$
$20 \times 2 = 40$

40 ✓
(1)
(Total for Question 2 is 2 marks)

3 Work out $24.1 - 1.79$

$$24.\overset{3}{\cancel{1}}\overset{10}{0}\overset{1}{} \\ -\ \ 1.79 \\ \overline{22.31}$$

22.31 ✓
(Total for Question 3 is 1 mark)

4 Write down the 15th odd number.

1, 3, 5, 7, 9, 11, 13, 15, 17, 19, 21, 23, 25, 27, 29

29 ✓
(Total for Question 4 is 1 mark)

5 $T = 3x + 2y$
$x = 5$
$y = 4$
Work out the value of T.

$T = 3(5) + 2(4)$
$= 15 + 8$ ✓

$T =$ 23 ✓
(Total for Question 5 is 2 marks)

6 Alan's wages are £240 each week.

He wants to save some money to buy a television.
The television costs £216.

Alan is going to save 10% of his wages each week.

How many weeks will it take Alan to save enough money to buy the television?

10% of 240 = £240 ÷ 10 = £24 ✓
24 × 10 = 240
24 × 9 = 240 − 24
= 216 ✓

9 ✓ weeks
(Total for Question 6 is 3 marks)

7 A rectangle is 4 cm by 8 cm.

Four of the rectangles are used to make a larger rectangle as shown below.

(a) Work out the perimeter of the larger rectangle.
Perimeter = 4 + 8 + 4 + 8 + 4 + 8 + 4 + 8 ✓
= 48 cm

48 ✓ cm
(2)

(b) Work out the area of the larger rectangle.
Length = 4 + 8 + 4 = 16 cm
Height = 8 cm ✓

Area = 16 × 8 = 128 cm²

128 ✓ cm²
(3)
(Total for Question 7 is 5 marks)

8 The diagram shows five towns.
It also shows the time it takes to drive between the towns.

Sue drives a delivery van.

She will start at A, and drive from A to B, then from B to C, then from C to D, then from D to E and from E back to A.

She will stop for 5 minutes in each town to make the delivery.
There is no delivery at A.
She wants to be back at A by 4 pm.

(a) What is the latest time Sue can start from A to make the deliveries then drive back to A by 4 pm?

A to B: 40 mins   B to C: 1 hour 10 mins

C to D: 1 hour   D to E: 30 mins

E to A: 50 mins

Stops in four towns for 5 minutes each:

4 × 5 = 20 mins ✓

Total: 2 hours + 150 mins = 4 hours 30 mins ✓

4 hours and 30 mins before 4 pm is 11.30 am.
✓

11.30 am ✓
(4)

Sue decides that she needs to reach E by 4 pm and does **not** need to return to A.

(b) Explain how this would affect the latest time Sue has to leave A.

Sue could leave A 50 minutes later because she would not need to drive back to A at the end. ✓
(1)
(Total for Question 8 is 5 marks)

9

The picture shows a lorry driver standing next to his lorry.
The lorry driver and the lorry are drawn to the same scale.

The lorry driver wants to drive the lorry into a car park.
The entrance to the car park is 3.1 metres high.

Can the lorry driver safely drive the lorry into the car park?
You must clearly show how you got your answer, explaining any
assumptions you have made.

Height of driver ≈ 1.8 m ✓

Height of lorry ≈ 2 × 1.8 = 3.6 m ✓

No. 3.6 m is more than 3.1 m. ✓

(Total for Question 9 is 3 marks)

5

10 Here are some cards.
The cards are labelled **X** or **Y**.

(a) What fraction of these cards are labelled **X**?
Give your fraction in its simplest form.

9 cards labelled X and 15 cards in total

Fraction labelled X = $\dfrac{9}{15}$ = $\dfrac{3}{5}$
✓

$\dfrac{3}{5}$ ✓

(2)

Tony takes some of these cards.
He takes cards labelled **X** and cards labelled **Y** in the ratio 2 : 1

(b) Work out the greatest number of cards labelled **Y** he could take.

Tony takes twice as many X as Y.

6Y and 12X (not possible) ✓

5Y and 10X (not possible)

4Y and 8X (possible)

The greatest number of cards labelled Y he could
take is 4.

4 ✓

(2)

(Total for Question 10 is 4 marks)

6

11 The table shows some information about the minimum and
maximum temperatures in Paris each month from January to May.
The temperatures are in °C.

	Jan	Feb	Mar	Apr	May
Minimum temperature	2	3	5	7	10
Maximum temperature	7	8	12	15	19

Show this information in a suitable diagram.

(Total for Question 11 is 4 marks)

7

12 Which is bigger, $\frac{2}{5}$ or 0.6?
Give a reason for your answer.

$\dfrac{2}{5} = \dfrac{4}{10} = 0.4$ ✓

0.4 < 0.6, so 0.6 is bigger than $\dfrac{2}{5}$ ✓

(Total for Question 12 is 2 marks)

8

133

13 Here are some coloured cards.

blue	red	blue	blue	green

red	green	blue	green	red

yellow	blue	yellow	red

A card is taken at random.

(a) Which colour of card is **most** likely to be taken?

Blue ✓

(1)

(b) What is the probability that the card is **red**?

4 red cards and 14 cards in total

Alternative acceptable answer:
$\frac{2}{7}$

$P(\text{Red}) = \frac{4}{14}$ ✓ ✓

(2)

James says:

"If there were two more green cards, then green would be the most likely colour of card to be taken."

(c) Is James right?

Give a reason for your answer.

There would be 3 + 2 = 5 green cards.

There are also 5 blue cards so green and blue

would be equally likely. James is not correct. ✓

(1)

(Total for Question 13 is 4 marks)

9

---

14 Maninder sold tickets for a concert.
She sold 895 tickets.

597 of these tickets were adult tickets.
The rest were child tickets.

Adult tickets were sold for £19.50 each.
Child tickets were sold for £9.75 each.

(a) Work out an estimate for the amount of money Maninder should receive for the tickets.

Adult tickets

$597 \times £19.50 \approx 600 \times £20 = £12\,000$ ✓

Child tickets

$895 - 597 \approx 900 - 600 = 300$ tickets sold

$300 \times £9.75 \approx 300 \times £10 = £3000$ ✓

$£3000 + £12\,000 = £15\,000$

£ 15 000 ✓

(3)

(b) Is your answer to part (a) an overestimate or an underestimate?
Give a reason for your answer.

Overestimate, because all values have been

rounded up. ✓

(1)
(Total for Question 14 is 4 marks)

10

---

15 Here are some white shapes and some grey shapes.

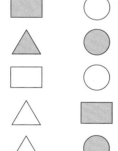

(a) What percentage of the shapes are white shapes?

5 white shapes and 10 shapes in total

$\frac{5}{10} \times 100\% = 50\%$

50 ✓ %

(1)

Ali takes some of the shapes.
$\frac{3}{7}$ of the shapes that are left are white shapes.

(b) How many white shapes and how many grey shapes did Ali take?

3 out of 7 shapes left are white. ✓

Ali took 2 white shapes and 3 shapes in total,

so she took 1 grey shape.

White shapes 2
Grey shapes ..... 1 ✓

(2)
(Total for Question 15 is 3 marks)

11

---

16 Work out 3.25×0.46

Estimate: $3 \times 0.5 = 1.5$

```
      3 2 5
×      4 6
    1 9 5 0
  1 3 0 0 0
  1 4 9 5 0  ✓ ✓
```

4 decimal places in question so add 4 decimal

places in answer: 1.4950

1.495 ✓

(Total for Question 16 is 3 marks)

12

17 Here is a diagram of a house.

The house is in the shape of a prism.

(a) On the grid, draw accurately the side elevation of the house from the direction marked with the arrow.

Use the scale 1 cm to represent 1 m.

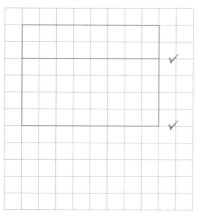

(2)

13

(b) On the grid below, draw accurately the plan of the house.

Use the scale 1 cm to represent 1 m.

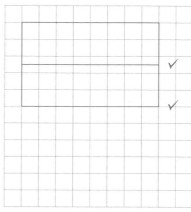

(2)

(Total for Question 17 is 4 marks)

14

18 The diagram represents the floor of a village hall.

The floor is in the shape of a rectangle.
The width is 10 m.
The length is 15 m.

The floor is going to be waxed.

1 litre of wax will cover 20 m² of floor.
The wax is sold in pots of 2 litres.
The cost of a pot of wax is £32.40.

All the wax has to be bought.
Work out the total cost of the pots of wax that have to be bought.
You must show how you got your answer.

Area of floor = 10 × 15 = 150 m² ✓

1 litre covers 20 m²

150 ÷ 20 = 15 ÷ 2 = 7.5 so you need 7.5 litres ✓

Each pot contains 2 litres so you need 4 pots

Total cost = 4 × £32.40 ✓

Estimate: 4 × £30 = £120

```
   3240
×     4
 12960
```
✓

Total cost = 129.60

£ 129.60 ✓

(Total for Question 18 is 5 marks)

15

19 The diagram below is drawn to scale and represents two cities on a map.

Scale: 1 cm represents 45 miles

(a) Work out the distance, in miles, between Lindun and Wrexmouth.

4 × 45 = 180 ✓

180 ✓ miles

(2)

Robert drove from Lindun to Wrexmouth.
He left Linden at 11 am.
He arrived at 2 pm.

Esther drove from Lindun to Northport.
She drove at the same speed as Robert.
She took 4 hours.

(b) Who travelled the greater distance and by how much?
You must show all your calculations.

Robert's speed = 180 ÷ 3 = 60 mph ✓

Esther drove 1 hour longer ✓

Esther drove the greater distance by 60 miles. ✓

(3)

(Total for Question 19 is 5 marks)

16

135

20 Here are the first four terms of a number sequence.

8   14   20   26
   +6   +6   +6

(a) Find an expression, in terms of n, for the nth term of this number sequence.

Zero term = 8 − 6 = 2 ✔

$6n + 2$ ✔

(2)

Dipen says:

"124 is a number in this sequence."

(b) Dipen is wrong.
Explain why.

$6n + 2 = 124$ $(−2)$

$6n = 122$

6 × 20 = 120 so 122 is not a multiple of 6 ✔

So n cannot be a whole number, so 124 is not a term in the sequence. ✔

(2)

The 100th term in this sequence is $5x + 2$

(c) Work out the value of x.

100th term = 6 × 100 + 2 ✔

$602 = 5x + 2$ $(−2)$

$600 = 5x$ $(÷5)$

$120 = x$

$x =$ 120 ✔

(2)

(Total for Question 20 is 6 marks)

17

21

ABC is an equilateral triangle.
AEF is a staight line.

$ACDE$ is a quadrilateral.
Angle $CDE = 100°$
Angle ACD is a right angle.

AE is parallel to BC.

Work out the size of the angle marked x.
Give reasons for each stage of your working.

Angle $BCA = 60°$ (Angles in an equilateral triangle are 60°) ✔

Angle $CAE = 60°$ (Alternate angles on parallel lines are equal)

360 − (90 + 60 + 100) = 360 − 250 = 110

Angle $AED = 110°$ (Angles in a quadrilateral add up to 360°) ✔

180 − 110 = 70

Angle $DEF = 70°$ (Angles on a straight line add up to 180°) ✔

$x =$ 70 ✔ °

(Total for Question 21 is 4 marks)

18

---

22 Here are three circles A, B and C.

The area of circle A is 200 cm².

The area of circle B is 15% larger than the area of circle A.

The area of circle C is 20% larger than the area of circle B.

How much larger is the area of circle C than the area of circle A?

15% of 200 cm² = 30 cm²

Area of B = 200 + 30 = 230 cm² ✔

20% of 230 cm² = 46 cm²

Area of C = 230 + 46 = 276 cm² ✔

276 − 200 = 76

C is bigger than A by 76 cm² ✔

(Total for Question 22 is 3 marks)

19

---

23 Martin's house has a meter to measure the amount of water he uses. Martin pays on Tariff A for the number of water units he uses.

The graph opposite can be used to find out how much he pays.

(a) (i) Find the gradient of this line.

Distance up = 47 − 15 = 32

Distance across = 100 − 20 = 80

Gradient $= \dfrac{32}{80} = \dfrac{4}{10} = 0.4$

0.4 ✔

(1)

Martin reduces the amount of water he uses by 15 units.

(ii) How much money does he save?

15 × 0.4 = 6

£ 6 ✔

(2)

Instead of Tariff A, Martin could pay for his water on Tariff B.

The table shows how much Martin would pay for his water on Tariff B.

Number of water units used	0	20	40	60	80	100
Cost in £	12	18	24	30	36	42

20

(b) (i) On the grid below, draw a line for Tariff B.

(ii) Write down the number of water units used when the cost of Tariff A is the same as the cost of Tariff B.

50 ✓ .... units

(3)

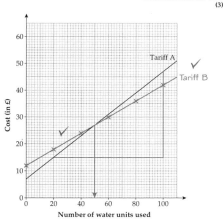

(Total for Question 23 is 6 marks)

TOTAL FOR PAPER IS 80 MARKS

21

137

Paper 2: Calculator
Time allowed: 1 hour 30 minutes

1 Simplify $3t + 6t - t$

8t ✓

(Total for Question 1 is 1 mark)

2 Simplify $e \times 4 \times f$

$4 \times e \times f$

4ef ✓

(Total for Question 2 is 1 mark)

3 Find the value of $\sqrt{(1.3)^3 - (0.79 \times 0.3)}$

1.4 ✓

(Total for Question 3 is 1 mark)

4 Simplify $6m + 3k - 2m + 5k$

$6m - 2m + 3k + 5k$ ✓

$4m + 8k$ ✓

(Total for Question 4 is 2 marks)

5 Simplify $y^4 \times y^3$

y^{4+3}

y^7 ✓

(Total for Question 5 is 1 mark)

6 5480 people are at a gig.
Each person has a ticket.
The ticket is coloured red or blue or yellow or green.

2074 people have a red ticket.
1459 people have a blue ticket.
$\frac{1}{3}$ of the rest of the people have a yellow ticket.

Work out how many people have a green ticket.

$5480 - 2074 - 1459 = 1947$ ✓

$1947 \div 3 = 649$ people have a yellow ticket ✓

$1947 - 649 = 1298$ have a green ticket

1298 ✓

(Total for Question 6 is 3 marks)

7 Sally makes a fair 8-sided spinner for a game.

Sally is going to spin the spinner once.
The spinner will land on one of the letters shown in the diagram.

| impossible   unlikely   evens   likely   certain |

From the list above, write down the word that best describes the likelihood:

(a) that the spinner will land on the letter Y

unlikely ✓

(1)

(b) that the spinner will land on the letter R

evens ✓

(1)

(c) that the spinner will land on the letter T.

impossible ✓

(1)

(Total for Question 7 is 3 marks)

8 Express 4 cm as a fraction of 2 m.
Write your fraction in its simplest form.

$2\,m = 200\,cm$

✓ $\dfrac{4}{200} \overset{\div 4}{\underset{\div 4}{=}} \dfrac{1}{50}$

$\dfrac{1}{50}$ ✓

(Total for Question 8 is 2 marks)

22

23

24

25

138

9 Charlotte, Samuel and Ben are given some money.

Samuel gets £7 more than Charlotte.
Ben gets twice as much as Samuel.
Together the three get a total of £69

Ben gives 35% of his share to charity.

Work out how much money Ben has left.

Charlotte: x

Samuel: $x + 7$

Ben: $2(x + 7)$

$$x + x + 7 + 2(x + 7) = 69 \quad ✓$$
$$4x + 21 = 69 \qquad (- 21)$$
$$4x = 48 \qquad (÷ 4)$$
$$x = 12 \quad ✓$$

Ben gets $2(x + 7) = 2 × 19 = £38$ ✓

$$\frac{65}{100} × £38 = £24.70$$

£ _____24.70_____ ✓

(Total for Question 9 is 4 marks)

10 Hafiz is going to cook a chicken.
The weight of the chicken is 2.5 kilograms.

The chicken has to be cooked for 20 minutes for each 500 grams of
its weight. He wants the chicken to finish cooking at 1 pm.

At what time should Hafiz start cooking the chicken?

$2500\,g = 5 × 500\,g$

$20 × 5 = 100$ minutes   ✓

$\qquad = 1$ hour and 40 minutes

1 pm − 1 hour = 12 noon

12 noon − 40 mins = 11:20 am   ✓

11:20 am   ✓

(3)

(Total for Question 10 is 3 marks)

11 Ayesha is making a fair 8-sided spinner.
The spinner already has the colours red, white and blue written on it.

The probability that the spinner lands on red will be $\frac{1}{2}$

The probability that the spinner lands on blue will be less than the
probability that the spinner lands on white.

Complete the spinner by writing on it the colours that are missing.

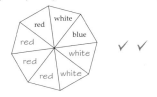   ✓   ✓

$P(\text{Red}) = \frac{1}{2}$ so 4 out of the 8 segments should be red.

$P(\text{Blue}) < P(\text{White})$ so there must be more white

segments than blue segments.

Alternative acceptable answer:

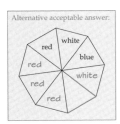

(Total for Question 11 is 2 marks)

12 Callum wins £300 in a raffle.

He gives 5% of the £300 to charity.

He saves $\frac{2}{5}$ of the £300

He uses the rest of the money to buy clothes.

Work out how much of the money Callum uses to buy clothes.

Charity

$\frac{5}{100} × 300 = 15$ ✓

Savings

$\frac{2}{5} × 300 = 120$ ✓

Clothes

$300 − 15 − 120 = 165$

£ _____165_____ ✓

(Total for Question 12 is 3 marks)

26

27

28

29

13 A book has puzzles graded easy, medium and hard.
Biran completes one of the easy puzzles in 35 seconds.

Biran says he can complete all 10 of the easy puzzles in under 6 minutes.

Is Biran correct?
You must show all your calculations and write down any assumptions you make.

$35 \times 10 = 350$ seconds

6 mins $= 360$ seconds

$350 < 360$ so Biran is correct. ✓

Assume that all puzzles take the same length of time to complete. ✓

> Alternative acceptable answer:
> Biran does not take a break between puzzles.

(Total for Question 13 is 2 marks)

---

14 The pie chart shows information about how the students in Year 11 get to school.

Mr Morley says: "Fewer than 10% of students in Year 11 get to school by car."

(a) Is Mr Morley correct?
You must explain your answer.

10% of the students would represent 10% of the circle. $360° \div 10 = 36°$. The 'car' sector is $40°$ which is larger than $36°$ ✓

so Mr Morley is not correct. ✓

(2)

50 students in Year 11 cycle to school.

(b) How many students in Year 11 walk to school?

Cycle sector $= 360° - 70° - 40° - 150°$

$= 100°$ ✓

$100° \div 50 = 2°$ so each student represents $2°$

Walk sector $= 150°$

$150° \div 2° = 75$

✓

.......75...✓...... students

(3)

(Total for Question 14 is 5 marks)

---

15 A shop sells tins of beans in three different sizes.

A   B   C

Kathy wants to buy exactly 750 g of beans.
She wants to buy the beans at the cheapest possible cost.

Work out the cheapest cost.
You must show all your working.

<u>1C + 3A</u>

$300\,g + 3 \times 150\,g = 750\,g$

$80p + 3 \times 35p = 185p$ ✓

<u>2C + 1A</u>

$2 \times 300\,g + 150\,g = 750\,g$

$2 \times 80p + 35p = 195p$

<u>3B + 1A</u>

$3 \times 200\,g + 150\,g = 750\,g$

$3 \times 45p + 35p = 170p$

<u>5A</u> ✓

$5 \times 150\,g = 750\,g$

$5 \times 35p = 175p$ ✓

The cheapest cost is 170p or £1.70

£..........1.70...✓.........

(Total for Question 15 is 4 marks)

---

16 Here is a knife.

$3x + 2$ $2x + 5$

All measurements are in centimetres.

The length of the handle is $3x + 2$
The length of the blade is $2x + 5$

The total length of the knife is 19 cm.

(a) Show that $5x + 7 = 19$

Total length $= 3x + 2 + 2x + 5 = 19$

$5x + 7 = 19$ ✓

(1)

(b) Solve $5x + 7 = 19$ (-7)

$5x = 12$ $(\div 5)$ ✓

$x = 2.4$

$x = $ ....2.4...✓..........

(2)

(Total for Question 16 is 3 marks)

17 You can use this conversion graph to change between miles and kilometres.

Mary has to drive from Paris to Calais, and then from Dover to Sheffield.
The total distance she has to drive is 350 miles.

Mary has already driven 240 km from Paris to the ferry at Calais.
She goes on a ferry to Dover.
She now has to drive from Dover to Sheffield.

Mary has enough petrol to drive 180 miles.

Will Mary have to stop for petrol on the way to Sheffield?

24 km = 15 miles ✓

240 km = 150 miles ✓

Remaining distance = 350 – 150 = 200 miles ✓

200 miles is more than 180 miles so Mary will have
to stop for petrol. ✓

(Total for Question 17 is 4 marks)

34

---

18 (a) Find two factors of 36 with a difference of 5

Factors of 36: 1 × 36, 2 × 18, 3 × 12,
                4 × 9, 6 × 6 ✓

.................1............ and ....6.... ✓

(2)

Alternative acceptable answer:

4 and 9.

The Lowest Common Multiple (LCM) of three numbers is 30
Two of the numbers are 2 and 5

(b) What could be the third number?

30 = 2 × 3 × 5 ✓

Alternative acceptable answers:

6, 15 and 30

.................3............ ✓

(2)

(Total for Question 18 is 4 marks)

35

---

19 Zoe asked a group of 25 friends to complete two puzzles.

The frequency polygon shows the times taken by each of her 25 friends to complete each puzzle.

(a) Write down what fraction of the group took between 4 minutes and 6 minutes to complete puzzle **A**.

$\dfrac{7}{25}$ ✓ ✓

(2)

(b) Which puzzle was harder?
Give a reason for your answer.

Only 1 person solved puzzle A in less than 2 minutes

7 people solved puzzle B in less than 2 minutes ✓

Puzzle A was harder ✓

Alternative acceptable answer:

Puzzle A: 7 + 8 + 6 = 21 friends took longer than
4 minutes to solve the puzzle
Puzzle B: 5 + 3 + 2 = 10 friends took longer
than 4 minutes to solve the puzzle
Puzzle A was harder

(2)

(Total for Question 19 is 4 marks)

36

20

ABC is a right-angled triangle.
Angle $B = 90°$
Angle $ACB = 22°$

P is a point on AB.
Q is a point on AC.
$AP = AQ$

Work out the size of angle APQ.
Give reasons for each stage of your working.

Angle $CAB = 180° – 90° – 22° = 68°$ ✓

(Angles in a triangle add up to 180°) ✓

Angle APQ = Angle AQP

(Base angles of an isosceles triangle are equal) ✓

So $x = (180° – 68°) ÷ 2 = 56°$ ✓

.................56.... ✓ °

(Total for Question 20 is 5 marks)

37

141

21 140 children will be at a school sports day.
Lily is going to give a cup of orange drink to each of the 140 children.
She is going to put 200 millilitres of orange drink in each cup.

The orange drink is made from orange squash and water.
The orange squash and water are mixed in the ratio 1 : 9 by volume.

Orange squash is sold in bottles containing 750 millilitres.

Work out how many bottles of orange squash Lily needs to buy.
You must show all your working.

140 × 200 = 28 000 ml of drink needed ✓

1 + 9 = 10 parts in ratio

28 000 ÷ 10 = 2800 ml of squash needed ✓

2800 ÷ 750 = 3.733... ✓

Lily needs to buy 4 bottles of squash. ✓

(Total for Question 21 is 4 marks)

22

ABCDE is a regular polygon.
EB is a straight line.
Angle *EBC* = 72°

Work out the size of the angle marked *x*.

Exterior angle = 360° ÷ 5 ✓

= 72°

x = 180° − 72° − 72° = 36° ✓

36 ✓ °

(Total for Question 22 is 3 marks)

23 *f* is inversely proportional to *d*.

When *d* = 50, *f* = 256

Find the value of *f* when *d* = 80

80 ÷ 50 = 1.6 ✓

d = 50   *f* = 256

× 1.6   ÷ 1.6 ✓

d = 80   *f* = 160

f = 160 ✓

(Total for Question 23 is 3 marks)

24

The diagram shows triangle *ABC*.
BC = 8.5 cm
Angle *ABC* = 90°
Angle *ACB* = 38°

Work out the length of *AB*.
Give your answer correct to 3 significant figures.

S^O_H C^A_H T^O_A

$\tan x = \dfrac{opp}{adj}$

$\tan 38° = \dfrac{AB}{8.5}$ ✓

AB = 8.5 × tan 38°

= 6.64092...

6.64 ✓ cm

(Total for Question 24 is 2 marks)

25 The front wheel of Jared's bicycle has a diameter of 55 cm.

(a) Work out the circumference of Jared's front wheel.
Give your answer correct to the nearest centimetre.

Circumference = π × diameter

= π × 55 ✓

= 172.787...

173 ✓ .... cm
(2)

Jared cycles 4.5 km to work each day.

(b) Work out the number of complete turns made by Jared's front wheel on his journey to work.

4.5 km = 4500 m = 450 000 cm

450 000 ÷ 172.787... = 2604.353...
✓

2604 ✓
(2)

Alternative acceptable answer:
450 000 ÷ 173 = 2601

(Total for Question 25 is 4 marks)

26 Henri and Ray buy some flowers for their mother.

They buy:
2 bunches of roses and 3 bunches of tulips for £10
1 bunch of roses and 4 bunches of tulips for £9.50.

(a) Work out the cost of one bunch of tulips.

$2r + 3t = 10$ (1)

$r + 4t = 9.5$ (2) ✓

$2 × (2):$ $2r + 8t = 19$

$− (1):$ $2r + 3t = 10$ ✓

$5t = 9$

$t = 1.8$ ✓

£ .... 1.80 ✓
(4)

Henri is 16 years old and Ray is 2 years younger than Henri.

They share the total cost of £19.50 in the ratio of their ages.

(b) Work out how much Henri pays and how much Ray pays.

16 : 14 = 8 : 7

8 + 7 = 15

£19.50 ÷ 15 = £1.30 ✓

Henri: 8 × £1.30 = £10.40

Ray: 7 × £1.30 = £9.10

Henri £ .... 10.40 ✓

Ray £ .... 9.10 ✓
(3)

(Total for Question 26 is 7 marks)

TOTAL FOR PAPER IS 80 MARKS

Paper 3: Calculator
Time allowed: 1 hour 30 minutes

1 Write the following numbers in order of size.
   Start with the smallest number.

   0.37   0.3   0.73   0.307

   0.3, 0.307, 0.37, 0.73 ✓

(Total for Question 1 is 1 mark)

2 Find the value of $(3.4 + 0.12)^3 = (3.52)^3$

   43.614 208 ✓

(Total for Question 2 is 1 mark)

3 (a) Solve $y \div 4 = 20$ $(\times 4)$
           $y = 20 \times 4$

   $y =$ ____80____ ✓
                              (1)

   (b) Solve $3x - 5 = 19$ $(+5)$
              $3x = 24$ $(\div 3)$ ✓
              $x = 8$

   $x =$ ____8____ ✓
                              (2)

(Total for Question 3 is 3 marks)

4 12 bags of cement cost £43.80.
   Work out the cost of 17 bags of cement.
   £43.80 ÷ 12 = £3.65
   £3.65 × 17 = £62.05
                        ✓

   £ ____62.05____ ✓

(Total for Question 4 is 2 marks)

5 Here is some information about the prices of four light switches.

   single switch   58p
   brass switch   £3.40
   double switch   £5.55
   dimmer switch   £7.82

   Buy two of the same switches and get the second half price.

   Martin buys:

        3 brass switches
        and 2 dimmer switches.

   He pays with a £50 note.

   How much change should he get?

   Cost of 3 brass switches = 2 × £3.40 + £1.70
                            = £8.50
   Cost of 2 dimmer switches = £7.82 + £3.91
                            = £11.73 ✓
   Total cost = £8.50 + £11.73 = £20.23
   Change = £50 – £20.23 = £29.77
                                    ✓

   £ ____29.77____ ✓

(Total for Question 5 is 3 marks)

6 Jim sells televisions.
   He keeps a record of the number of televisions he sells each week.

   The table gives some information about the number of each make of television he sold last week.

   | | Make of television | | |
	Sandi	Bish	Ebo
Monday	4	2	1
Tuesday	3	4	2
Wednesday	0	3	1
Thursday	0	5	2
Friday	1	1	1
Saturday	4	5	3
Total:	12	20	10	✓

   Jim's shop is closed on Sunday.

   The table below gives information about the cost of each television.

   | | Make of television | | |
	Sandi	Bish	Ebo
Cost	£129	£149	£169

   Jim is paid a bonus when all the televisions he sells in a week have a total cost of £6000 or more.

   Will Jim be paid a bonus for last week?

   12 × £129 + 20 × £149 + 10 × £169 = £6218 ✓
                                          ✓
   £6218 > £6000 so Jim will be paid a bonus. ✓

(Total for Question 6 is 4 marks)

7   Jake makes a picture frame from 4 identical pieces of card.
Each piece of card is in the shape of a trapezium.

8 cm   12 cm

The outer edge of the frame is a square of side 12 cm.
The inner edge of the frame is a square of side 8 cm.

Work out the area of each piece of card.

Area of 4 pieces = $12^2 - 8^2$ ✓

    = 144 − 64

    = 80   ✓

80 ÷ 4 = 20

    ✓

20 ✓ .... cm²

(Total for Question 7 is 4 marks)

---

8   Jane helps to organise a dance group.
The dancers use sticks in some of the dances.

Jane needs some ribbon to tie on the sticks.
She needs to buy enough ribbon for 20 sticks.

Each stick has 8 pieces of ribbon.
Each piece of ribbon is 30 cm long.

The ribbon is sold in rolls.
Each roll has 25 m of ribbon.

How many rolls of ribbon does Jane need to buy?

For one stick: 8 × 30 = 240 cm

For 20 sticks: 20 × 240 = 4800 cm = 48 m   ✓

    ✓

Jane will need to buy 2 rolls.   ✓

(Total for Question 8 is 3 marks)

---

9   James thinks of a number.

He multiplies his number by 8
He subtracts 7 from the result.

His answer is 89

What number did James think of?

? — ×8 — −7 → 89
    ÷8 — +7

    ✓

89 + 7 = 96

96 ÷ 8 = 12

The number was 12   ✓

(Total for Question 9 is 2 marks)

---

10 Mike is a school caretaker.
He is marking out the positions of some posts in the school yard.

The cross at *B* shows the position for a basketball post.

Mike is going to put a netball post at the point (3, 0).

Mike wants to paint a spot on the yard exactly halfway between
the two posts.

Work out the coordinates of the position of the spot.

(5 ✓ , 3 ✓)

(Total for Question 10 is 2 marks)

48

49

50

51

145

11 This formula is used to work out the body mass index, B, for a person of mass M kg and height H metres.

$$B = \frac{M}{H^2}$$

A person with a body mass index between 25 and 30 is overweight.

Arthur has a mass of 96 kg.
He has a height of 2 metres.

Is Arthur overweight?
You must show all your working.

$B = \dfrac{M}{H^2} = \dfrac{96}{2^2} = \dfrac{96}{4} = 24$ ✓
✓

Arthur is not overweight. ✓

(Total for Question 11 is 3 marks)

---

12 Gary recorded the number of eggs in each of 10 nests.
Here are his results.

1   1   2   2   2   2   3   3   3   4

(a) Write down the mode.

2 ✓

(1)

(b) Work out the mean.

$1 + 1 + 2 + 2 + 2 + 2 + 3 + 3 + 3 + 4 = 23$

$23 \div 10 = 2.3$
✓

2.3 ✓

(2)

(c) Which best describes the average numbers of eggs in these nests, the mode or the mean?
Give a reason for your answer.

The mode, because it gives a whole number
of eggs. ✓

(1)

Alternative acceptable answer:

The mean, because it takes into account all
the values.

(Total for Question 12 is 4 marks)

---

13 Colin makes and sells chocolates.
Here is information about his profits for the past two years.

	Jan–Jun	Jul–Dec
2013	£5000	£5400
2014	£5600	£7800

Colin writes this statement in his report:
'My total profit in 2014 is 40% more than my total profit in 2013'.

(a) Is this statement correct?
You must show all your working.

2013: £5000 + £5400 = £10 400
2014: £5600 + £7800 = £13 400 ✓

£10 400 × 1.4 = £14 560 ✓

£13 400 < £14 560

Colin's 2014 profit was less than 40% more than
his 2013 profit. He is not correct. ✓

(3)

Colin says that in 2015 he should make a total profit of £16 400

(b) What assumptions has Colin made?

Colin has assumed his profit will increase by the
same amount (£3000) from 2014 to 2015 as it
did from 2013 to 2014. ✓

(1)

(Total for Question 13 is 4 marks)

14

A, B, C and D are points on a straight line.
$AD = 40$ cm
$AB = 8$ cm
$BC = CD$

Explain why $AB : CD = 1 : 2$

$BD = 40 - 8 = 32$ cm ✓

$BC = CD$ so each section is half of BD.

$32 \div 2 = 16$, so $CD = 16$ cm ✓

So $AB : CD = 8 : 16 = 1 : 2$ ✓
✓

(Total for Question 14 is 4 marks)

15

The diagram shows two congruent triangles and a square.

Find the size of the angle marked x.

Angles in a triangle add up to 180°

Missing angles in triangles = 180° − (37° + 66°)

= 77° ✓

x = 360° − (77° + 77° + 90°) = 116°
✓

x = ...116... ✓ °

(Total for Question 15 is 3 marks)

16   You can use this conversion to change between pounds (£) and dollars ($).

£25 = $40

Stacey bought a watch in New York.
The watch cost $220

In London, the same type of watch costs £140

Compare the cost of the watch in New York with the cost of the watch in London.

$220 = $\frac{220}{40}$ × 25 ✓

= £137.50 < £140 ✓

So the watch is cheaper in New York. ✓

(Total for Question 16 is 3 marks)

17   Kelvin and Mamady are in the same class.
The probability that Kelvin arrives on time is 0.7
The probability that Mamady arrives on time is 0.9

Complete the probability tree diagram.

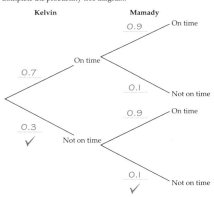

(Total for Question 17 is 2 marks)

18   £360 is shared in the ratio 1 : 3 : 5

Work out the difference between the largest share and the smallest share.

1 + 3 + 5 = 9

£360 ÷ 9 = £40 ✓

5 × £40 = £200

£200 − £40 = £160
✓

£ ....160... ✓

(Total for Question 18 is 3 marks)

19 The heights (in cm) of 13 girls and 13 boys were recorded.

The back-to-back stem-and-leaf diagram gives this information.

				girls			boys			
			9	8	14					
			4	2	15	7	9			
8	4	(4)	2	0	16	2	6	8	9	
	9	5	3	0	17	(0)	3	4	6	6
					18	1	4			

KEY:
8 | 14 represents a height   15 | 7 represents a height
of 148 cm for girls   of 157 cm for boys

Compare the distribution of the heights of the girls and the distribution of the heights of the boys.

Girls' range = 179 − 148 = 31 cm
Boys' range = 184 − 157 = 27 cm
Girls' median = 164 cm
Boys' median = 170 cm ✓
Girls' heights are more spread out than the boys'
(31 cm > 27 cm). ✓
Girls were shorter on average (164 cm < 170 cm). ✓

(Total for Question 19 is 3 marks)

20 A number is increased by 25% to get 5950

What is the number?

100% + 25% = 125% ✓

$$\frac{125\%}{100\%} = 1.25$$

5950 ÷ 1.25 = 4760
✓

4760 ✓

(Total for Question 20 is 3 marks)

21 Here is a list of ingredients for making small cakes.

Small cakes

400 g flour
200 g butter
200 g sugar
   2 eggs

Makes 15 small cakes

Rosie has

2 kg   of flour
800 g   of butter
1.5 kg of sugar
12   eggs

What is the greatest number of small cakes Rosie can make?

You must show all your working.

Flour: 2000 ÷ 400 = 5
Butter: 800 ÷ 200 = 4 ✓
Sugar: 1500 ÷ 200 = 7.5
Eggs: 12 ÷ 2 = 6 ✓
4 batches = 4 × 15 = 60 small cakes
✓

60 ✓

(Total for Question 21 is 4 marks)

22 Savio has two fair dice.
He throws the two dice and adds the scores together.

(a) What is the probability of getting a total of exactly 11?

	1	2	3	4	5	6
1	2	3	4	5	6	7
2	3	4	5	6	7	8
3	4	5	6	7	8	9
4	5	6	7	8	9	10
5	6	7	8	9	10	11
6	7	8	9	10	11	12 ✓

Alternative acceptable answer:
$\frac{1}{18}$

$P(11) = \frac{2}{36}$ ✓ ✓

(3)

(b) What total score is Savio most likely to get?

7 ✓

(1)

Savio says:

"The probability of getting a total of 5 or more is $\frac{3}{4}$."

(c) Is Savio correct?
You must show your working.

$P(5 \text{ or more}) = \frac{30}{36}$

$\frac{3}{4} = \frac{27}{36}$ ✓

So Savio is incorrect. ✓

(2)

(Total for Question 22 is 6 marks)

23 (a) Complete the table of values for $y = x^2 - 3x + 1$ ✓

x	−1	0	1	2	3	4
y	5	1	−1	−1	1	5

✓   ✓

$x = -1: y = (-1)^2 - 3(-1) + 1 = 1 + 3 + 1 = 5$
$x = 1: y = (1)^2 - 3(1) + 1 = 1 - 3 + 1 = -1$
$x = 2: y = (2)^2 - 3(2) + 1 = 4 - 6 + 1 = -1$

(2)

(b) Draw the graph of $y = x^2 - 3x + 1$ for values of x from −1 to 4

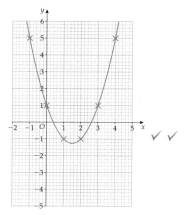

✓ ✓

(2)

(Total for Question 23 is 4 marks)

64

24 Caroline is making some table decorations.
Each decoration is made from a candle
and a holder.

Caroline buys some candles and some
holders each in packs.

There are 30 candles in a pack of candles.
There are 18 holders in a pack of holders.

Caroline buys exactly the same number of
candles and holders.

candle and
holder

(a) What is the smallest number of packs of candles and holders
that Caroline can buy?

Number of packs	1	2	3	4	5
Number of candles	30	60	(90)	120	150
Number of holders	18	36	54	72	(90)

✓

3 ✓ .... packs of candles
5 ✓ .... packs of holders
(3)

Caroline uses all her candles and all her holders.

(b) How many table decorations does Caroline make?

90 ✓ .... table decorations
(1)

(Total for Question 24 is 4 marks)

65

25 Solve $x^2 - 2x - 24 = 0$

$x^2 - 2x - 24 = 0$
$(x - 6)(x + 4) = 0$ ✓

$x = 6 \quad x = -4$

$x = 6$ ✓ or $x = -4$ ✓

(Total for Question 25 is 3 marks)

26 $a = \begin{pmatrix} -3 \\ -2 \end{pmatrix}$ $\qquad$ $b = \begin{pmatrix} 5 \\ -1 \end{pmatrix}$

Work out $a - 3b$ as a column vector

$\begin{pmatrix} -3 \\ -2 \end{pmatrix} - 3 \begin{pmatrix} 5 \\ -1 \end{pmatrix} = \begin{pmatrix} -3 - 3(5) \\ -2 - 3(-1) \end{pmatrix}$

 ✓ ✓

(Total for Question 26 is 2 marks)

TOTAL FOR PAPER IS 80 MARKS

66

149

Paper 1: Non-calculator
Time allowed: 1 hour 30 minutes

1 (a) There were 5781 people at a football match.
Write down the value of the 8 in the number 5781

> Alternative acceptable answer:
> 8 tens

80 ✓
(1)

(b) The length of a nail is 1.76 cm.
Write down the value of the 7 in 1.76

> Alternative acceptable answer:
> 7 tenths

$\frac{7}{10}$ ✓
(1)
(Total for Question 1 is 2 marks)

2 (a) Annabel's thumb is 2.5 centimetres long.
Change 2.5 centimetres to millimetres.

2.5×10

25 ✓
............mm
(1)

(b) There are 450 millilitres of water in a jug.
Change 450 millilitres to litres.

$450 \div 1000$

0.45 ✓
............litres
(1)
(Total for Question 2 is 2 marks)

67

3 Write down $\frac{23}{1000}$ as a decimal.

$0.\overset{\frown}{023}$

0.023 ✓
(Total for Question 3 is 1 mark)

4 Find four different prime numbers you can add together to get a number greater than 30 and less than 40

2, 3, 5, 7, 11, 13, 17, 19 ✓

$5 + 7 + 11 + 13 = 36$

> Alternative acceptable answer:
> Any four different prime numbers with a sum between 31 and 39

5   7   11   13 ✓
(Total for Question 4 is 2 marks)

68

5 Mary buys three tickets for a theatre show.
Each ticket costs £49.50 plus booking fee.

The booking fee is £2.25 per ticket.

Mary has £150 in her purse.

Does she have enough money to pay for the total cost of the tickets?

$3 \times £49.50 = £148.50$ ✓

$2.25 \times 3 = 6.75$

$\begin{array}{r} 148.50 \\ + \quad 6.75 \\ \hline 155.25 \end{array}$ ✓

The total cost is £155.25. She does not have enough money. ✓

(Total for Question 5 is 3 marks)

69

6 $K = 3h^2 - j$
$h = -6$
$j = 8$
Work out the value of K.

$K = 3 \times (-6)^2 - 8$
$\quad = 3 \times 36 - 8$ ✓
$\quad = 108 - 8$

$K =$ 100 ✓
(Total for Question 6 is 2 marks)

70

7 A company sells toy cars.
The company has 5 cars left to sell.

    2 of the cars are blue.
    3 of the cars are red.

Carl buys a toy car.
The company picks the toy car at random.

(a) On the probability scale, mark with a cross (×) the probability that Carl gets a yellow car.

                  ✓

(1)

(b) On the probability scale, mark with a cross (×) the probability that Carl gets a blue car.

                  ✓

(1)

(c) There are some boys and girls in a nursery.

The probability of choosing a girl at random is $\frac{4}{7}$

What is the probabilty of choosing a boy?

$1 - \frac{4}{7} = \frac{3}{7}$

              $\frac{3}{7}$ ✓

(1)

(Total for Question 7 is 3 marks)

71

---

8 Jim is an IT consultant.

Jim is paid at his normal rate of pay from Monday to Friday.
On a Saturday he is paid 1.5 times his normal rate.
On a Sunday he is paid twice his normal rate.

One week he works 7 days for a company.
He is paid £400 for 25 hours of work from Monday to Friday.
He works for 6 hours on Saturday.
He works for 3 hours on Sunday.

Does he earn enough money this week to pay for a deposit of £650 for a car?
You must show all your working.

$400 \div 25 = 1600 \div 100 = 16$ ✓

Jim earns £16 per hour during the week.

Saturday

$16 \times 1.5 = 16 + 8 = 24$

$6 \times 24 = 144$ ✓

Sunday

$16 \times 2 = 32$

$3 \times 32 = 96$ ✓

Total

   400
   144
+ 96
   640 ✓

Jim earns £640 so he does not earn enough money to pay for the deposit. ✓

(Total for Question 8 is 5 marks)

72

---

9 David takes, at random, a number from Box A.
He then takes, at random, a letter from Box B.

     Box A   **Box B**

  1   2   A
               C
    6   E

(a) List all the possible outcomes he could get.

1A, 1C, 1E, 2A, 2C, 2E, 6A, 6C, 6E ✓
           ✓

(2)

(b) Find the probability that David takes the number 2 and the letter E.

             $\frac{1}{9}$ ✓

(1)

(c) Find the probability that David picks the letter C.

Alternative acceptable answer:
$\frac{1}{3}$

             $\frac{3}{9}$ ✓

(1)

(Total for Question 9 is 4 marks)

73

---

10 Here are the first four terms in a number sequence.

  5   8   11   14   17, 20, 23, 26, 29, 32, 35
    +3   +3   +3   ✓

Kasey thinks that the number 34 is in this sequence.

Is Kasey correct?
You must show how you get your answer.

No. 34 is not in the sequence. ✓

Alternative acceptable answer:
nth term = $3n + 2$
$3n + 2 = 34$
$3n = 32$
$n = 10\frac{2}{3}$
n not a whole number
so 34 is not a term
in the sequence.

(Total for Question 10 is 2 marks)

74

151

11 Which of these fractions is the larger?

$\frac{1}{3}$ or $\frac{2}{5}$

You must show clearly how you got your answer.

$\frac{6}{15} > \frac{5}{15}$ so $\frac{2}{5} > \frac{1}{3}$ ✓

Alternative acceptable answer:
$\frac{1}{3} = 0.333...$ and $\frac{2}{5} = 0.4$
so $\frac{2}{5}$ is larger

(Total for Question 11 is 2 marks)

75

12 Here is the sketch of a garden.

Draw an accurate diagram of the garden.
Use a scale of 1 cm represents 1 m.
The side *AB* has already been drawn for you.

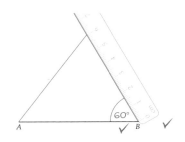

(Total for Question 12 is 2 marks)

76

13 Sherri says:

"If you multiply an odd number by 7 and take away 2, you always get a prime number."

Show that Sherri is wrong.

$5 \times 7 - 2 = 35 - 2 = 33$ ✓

33 is not prime because $11 \times 3 = 33$

So Sherri is wrong. ✓

(Total for Question 13 is 2 marks)

77

14 Write these numbers in order of size.
Start with the smallest number.

$0.6 \qquad \frac{2}{3} \qquad 65\% \qquad 0.606$

$\frac{2}{3} = 0.66666...$

$65\% = 0.65$ ✓

Order is 0.6, 0.606, 0.65, 0.6666...

$0.6, 0.606, 65\%, \frac{2}{3}$ ✓

(Total for Question 14 is 2 marks)

78

152

15

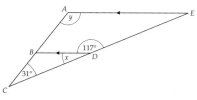

AE is parallel to *BD*.
ABC and *CDE* are straight lines.

(a) (i) Work out the size of the angle marked *x*.

$180° − 117° = 63°$

$x = $ ....63....✓... °
(1)

(ii) Give a reason for your answer.

Angles on a straight line add up to 180° ✓

....
(1)

(b) (i) Work out the size of the angle marked *y*.

$180° − (31° + 63°) = 180° − 94° = 86°$ ✓

$y = $ ....86....✓... °

(ii) Give the reasons for your answer.

Angle *CBD* = *y*° (Corresponding angles are equal)
Angles in a triangle add up to 180° ✓
(3)

(Total for Question 15 is 5 marks)

79

16

A model of a space shuttle is made to a scale of 2.5 centimetres to 1 metre.
The length of the space shuttle is 30 metres.

(a) Work out the length of the model.
Give your answer in centimetres.

$30 × 2.5 = 75$ ✓

.......75....✓... cm
(2)

The height of the model is 12.5 centimetres.

(b) Work out the height of the space shuttle.
Give your answer in metres.

$12.5 ÷ 2.5 = 5$ ✓

.......5....✓... m
(2)

(Total for Question 16 is 4 marks)

80

17 A machine makes 36 trophies every hour.

The machine makes trophies for $8\frac{1}{2}$ hours each day, on 5 days of the week.

The trophies are packed into boxes.
Each box holds 8 trophies.

How many boxes are needed for all the trophies made each week?

$36 × 8\frac{1}{2}$

$\begin{array}{r} 36 \\ × \ \ 8 \\ \hline 288 \\ {\scriptstyle 4} \end{array}$

$\frac{1}{2}$ of 36 = 18

288 + 18 = 306 trophies per day ✓

$\begin{array}{r} 306 \\ × \ \ \ 5 \\ \hline 1530 \\ {\scriptstyle 3} \end{array}$ ✓

1530 trophies per week

$\begin{array}{r} 1\ 9\ 1 \ \text{remainder 2} \\ 8 \overline{)\ 15^7 3^1 0} \end{array}$
✓

.......192....✓... boxes

(Total for Question 17 is 4 marks)

18 Expand and simplify

$(x + 4)(x + 6) = x^2 + 6x + 4x + 24$ ✓

$\qquad\qquad = x^2 + 10x + 24$

$x^2 + 10x + 24$ ✓

(Total for Question 18 is 2 marks)

81

19 Here is some information about a cricket and tennis club.

80 people belong to the club.
35 play cricket.
50 play tennis.
15 play both cricket and tennis.

(a) Draw a Venn diagram to show this information.

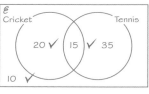

$50 − 15 = 35$
$35 − 15 = 20$
$20 + 15 + 35 = 70$
$80 − 70 = 10$

(4)

One of the people who belongs to the club is chosen at random.

(b) Work out the probability that this person does not play cricket or tennis.

Alternative acceptable answers:
$\frac{5}{40}, \frac{1}{8}$ or 0.125

$\frac{10}{80}$ ✓
(2)

(Total for Question 19 is 6 marks)

82

153

20 Mark works for 5 days each week.

Mark can travel to work by car or train.

By car
He travels a total distance of 24 miles each day
His car travels 30 miles per gallon
Diesel costs £1.50 per litre

By train
Weekly pass costs £25.75

1 gallon = 4.5 litres

Is it more expensive if he uses his car or the train?

You must show your working.

<u>Total distance</u>

24 × 5 = 120 miles ✓

<u>Diesel used</u>

120 ÷ 30 = 4 gallons

4 × 4.5 = 18 litres ✓

<u>Cost of diesel</u>

18 × £1.50 = £27 ✓

£27 is more than £25.75 so his car is more

expensive. ✓

(Total for Question 20 is 4 marks)

83

---

21 (a) Complete the table of values for $y = x^3 - 4x$

x	-3	-2	-1	0	1	2	3
y	-15	0	3	0	-3	0	15

✓

(2)

$(-3)^3 - 4(-3) = -27 + 12 = -15$

$(-2)^3 - 4(-2) = -8 + 8 = 0$

$(1)^3 - 4(1) = 1 - 4 = -3$

$(2)^3 - 4(2) = 8 - 8 = 0$

(b) On the grid, draw the graph of $y = x^3 - 4x$ from $x = -3$ to $x = 3$

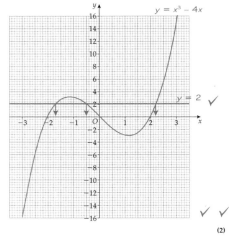

(2)

(c) Use your graph to find estimates of the solutions to the equation
$x^3 - 4x = 2$

$x = -1.7, \ x = -0.5, \ x = 2.2$ ✓

(2)

(Total for Question 21 is 6 marks)

84

---

22 Jean makes a metal structure out of steel rope.

The diagram below shows the metal structure.

The two circles are identical.

The diameter of each circle is 2.5 metres.

Show that the total length of the steel rope used to make the metal structure is $(a + b\pi)$ metres where a and b are integers.

Length of diagonal $= \sqrt{12^2 + 5^2} = \sqrt{169} = 13$ ✓

Wire used on diagonal $= 13 - 2.5 - 2.5 = 8$ ✓

Circumference of each circle $= \pi \times 2.5$ ✓

Total length of wire

$= 12 + 5 + 8 + 2.5\pi + 2.5\pi = 25 + 5\pi$ ✓

✓

(Total for Question 22 is 5 marks)

85

23

Find y.

$2y + 3y + 20 + y + 10 = 6y + 30$ ✓

$6y + 30 = 180$ ✓ (-30) $6\overline{)15^30}$ $= 25$

$6y = 150$ $(÷6)$

$y = 25$

$y =$ 25 ✓ °

(3)

(Total for Question 23 is 3 marks)

86

24 Asha wants to buy a mobile phone.

She finds an online shop that has a sale that offers 20% of all mobile phones.

On Black Friday, the online shop reduces all sale prices on mobile phones by a further 30%.

Asha buys a mobile phone on Black Friday.

Work out the final percentage reduction that Asha receives on the price of the mobile phone.

Multiplier for 20% reduction is × 0.8

Multiplier for 30% reduction is × 0.7 ✓

8 × 7 = 56 so 0.8 × 0.7 = 0.56 ✓

1 − 0.56 = 0.44 ✓

0.44 × 100 = 44%

_____44_____ ✓ %

(Total for Question 24 is 4 marks)

87

25 A and B are straight lines.
Line A has the equation $3y = 2x + 8$
Line B goes through the points $(-1, 2)$ and $(2, 8)$

Do lines A and B intersect?
You must show your working

<u>Line A</u>
$y = \frac{2}{3}x + \frac{8}{3}$
Gradient = $\frac{2}{3}$ ✓

<u>Line B</u>

(2, 8)

6

(−1, 2)

3

Gradient = 2 ✓

The lines are not parallel so they do intersect. ✓

(Total for Question 25 is 3 marks)

TOTAL FOR PAPER IS 80 MARKS

88

155

Paper 2: Calculator
Time allowed: 1 hour 30 minutes

1 Simplify $3 \times c \times d$

$3cd$ ✓

(Total for Question 1 is 1 mark)

2 Simplify $3x + 7y + 2x - y = 3x + 2x + 7y - y$

✓ ✓
$5x + 6y$

(Total for Question 2 is 2 marks)

3 Expand $t(3t^2 + 4)$

$t \times 3t^2$

$t \times 4$ ✓

$3t^3 + 4t$ ✓

(Total for Question 3 is 2 marks)

4 Write 178% as a decimal.

$178 \div 100 = 1.78$

1.78 ✓

(Total for Question 4 is 1 mark)

89

5 Here is the menu in Sam's Cafe.

Sam's Cafe	
cup of tea	£1.20
cup of coffee	£1.40
breakfast: sausage, eggs, bacon	£4.10
special: sausage, eggs, bacon and toast	£4.50

Sameena buys some cups of coffee.
She only has £10

(a) Work out the greatest number of cups of coffee she can buy.

$10 \div 1.4 = 7.1428....$
✓

7 ✓ cups
(2)

A child's meal costs half of the cost of the special.

(b) Work out the cost of a child's meal.

$4.5 \div 2 = 2.25$

£ 2.25 ✓
(1)

(Total for Question 5 is 3 marks)

90

6 Jack makes a fair 6-sided spinner for a game.

Jack will spin the spinner once.
The spinner will land on one of the numbers.

(a) Draw a circle around the word that best describes the probability of this event.

The spinner will land on 3

impossible	unlikely	evens	likely	certain

✓
(1)

Jack makes a different fair 6-sided spinner.
The spinner only has the numbers 1, 2 and 3 on it.

The probability that the spinner will land on 1 is $\frac{1}{2}$

The probability that the spinner will land on 2 is greater than the probability that the spinner will land on 3

(b) Write the numbers on the spinner.

✓ ✓
(2)

(Total for Question 6 is 3 marks)

91

7 Work out the value of $4x^3$ when $x = 2$

$4 \times (2)^3 = 4 \times 8 = 32$

32 ✓

(Total for Question 7 is 1 mark)

8 Make c the subject of the formula $a = b + 5c$ $(-b)$

$a - b = 5c$ $(\div 5)$ ✓

$\frac{a - b}{5} = c$

$c = \frac{a - b}{5}$ ✓

(Total for Question 8 is 2 marks)

92

156

9 Solve $4m + 6 = 15$ (-6)

$\qquad 4m = 9$ $(\div 4)$ ✓

$\qquad m = 9 \div 4$

$m = \underline{\quad 2.25 \quad}$ ✓

(Total for Question 9 is 2 marks)

93

---

10 A box containing screws weighs 1.21 kilograms.
Each screw weighs 2.5 grams.
When empty, the box weighs 60 grams.

Sandeep says: "The number of screws in the box is 460."
Is Sandeep correct? You must show your working.

$460 \times 2.5 = 1150$ ✓

$1150 + 60 = 1210\,g$ ✓

$1210\,g$ ✓ $= 1.21\,kg$ so Sandeep is correct. ✓

Alternative acceptable answer:

$1.21\,kg = 1210\,g$

$1210 - 60 = 1150$

$1150 \div 2.5 = 460$ so Sandeep is correct.

(Total for Question 10 is 4 marks)

94

11

ABC is a straight line.
Angle $BCD = 38°$
The reflex angle $BDC = 250°$
Work out the size of the angle marked x.
Give reasons for your answer.

Angle $CDB = 360° - 250° = 110°$

(Angles around a point add up to 360°) ✓

Angle $CBD = 180° - 38° - 110° = 32°$

(Angles in a triangle add up to 180°) ✓

$x = 180° - 32° = 148°$

(Angles on a straight line add up to 180°)

$x = \underline{\quad 148 \quad}$ ✓ °

(Total for Question 11 is 4 marks)

95

---

12 Amy is making a shelf unit for her DVDs.

She needs:

     3 pieces of wood of length 32 cm
and 2 pieces of wood of length 45 cm.

Amy has a piece of wood of length 2 metres.
She cuts the 5 pieces of wood she needs from the 2 metre length of wood.

(a) What length of wood does Amy have left from the 2 metre length?

$3 \times 32 = 96$

$2 \times 45 = 90$

$96 + 90 = 186$ ✓

$2\,m = 200\,cm$

$200 - 186 = 14$

✓

$\underline{\quad 14\,cm \quad}$ ✓

(3)

The diagram shows the shelf unit.

Amy will put DVDs on the 2 shelves, as shown in the diagram.
Each DVD has a width of 14 mm.

(b) What is the greatest number of DVDs Amy can put on the 2 shelves?

$320 \div 14 = 22.85...$ ✓

$22 \times 2 = 44$

✓

$\underline{\quad 44 \quad}$ ✓ DVDs

(3)

(Total for Question 12 is 6 marks)

96

157

13 Alan, Ben and Clara are playing a card game.

Alan has p cards.
Ben has twice as many cards as Alan.
Clara has 3 cards fewer than Ben.

They have a total of 17 cards.

Work out how many cards each person has.

Alan $= p$
Ben $= 2p$
Clara $= 2p - 3$
Total $= p + 2p + 2p - 3 = 5p - 3$ ✓

$5p - 3 = 17$ $\quad (+3)$ ✓
$\quad 5p = 20$ $\quad (\div 5)$
$\quad\quad p = 4$

Alan: ....4........ cards ✓✓
Ben: ....8........ cards
Clara: ....5........ cards

(Total for Question 13 is 4 marks)

97

14 There are 200 counters in a bag.
The counters are blue or red or yellow.

$\frac{1}{4}$ of the counters are blue.

$\frac{2}{5}$ of the counters are red.

Work out the number of yellow counters in the bag.

Blue $= \frac{1}{4} \times 200 = 50$ ✓
Red $= \frac{2}{5} \times 200 = 80$ ✓
Yellow $= 200 - 50 - 80 = 70$
✓

.........70......... ✓

(Total for Question 14 is 4 marks)

98

15 Here is the number of goals scored by a football team in each of its first 10 games.

3   1   4   2   0   1   1   1   3   2

(a) Write down the mode.

.........1......... ✓

(1)

(b) Work out the mean number of goals for the first 10 games.

$3 + 1 + 4 + 2 + 0 + 1 + 1 + 1 + 3 + 2 = 18$
$18 \div 10 = 1.8$
✓

.........1.8......... ✓

(2)

In the 11th game the team scored 4 goals.
In the 12th game the team scored 2 goals.

(c) Will the mean number of goals for the 12 games be greater than or less than the mean number of goals for the first 10 games? You must explain your answer.

 Greater, because both values are higher than the mean for the first 10 games. ✓

(2)

(Total for Question 15 is 5 marks)

99

16 A baker makes jam rolls.

The baker uses flour, butter and jam in the ratio 8 : 4 : 5 to make jam rolls.

The table shows the cost per kilogram of some of these ingredients.

Cost per kilogram	
Flour	40p
Butter	£2.50
Jam	£1.00

The total weight of the flour, butter and jam for each jam roll is 425 g.

The baker wants to make 200 jam rolls. He has £90 to spend on the ingredients.

Does he have enough money?
You must show your working.

$8 + 4 + 5 = 17$
$425 \div 17 = 25$ ✓

1 jam roll

Flour: $8 \times 25 = 200\,g$ ✓
Butter: $4 \times 25 = 100\,g$
Jam: $5 \times 25 = 125\,g$

200 jam rolls

Flour: $0.2 \times 200 \times 0.4 = £16$ ✓
Butter: $0.1 \times 200 \times 2.50 = £50$
Jam: $0.125 \times 200 \times 1 = £25$
$16 + 50 + 25 = £91$ ✓

He does not have enough money. ✓

(Total for Question 16 is 5 marks)

100

158

17 There are 130 adults at a language school.
Each adult studies either French or Spanish or German.

96 of the adults are women.
12 of the women study French.
73 of the adults study Spanish.
55 of the women study Spanish.
9 of the men study German.

(a) Complete the two-way table.

	French	Spanish	German	Total
Men	7	18	9	34
Women	12	55	29	96
Total	19	73	38	130

✓ ✓ ✓ (3)

(b) One adult is chosen at random.
Work out the probability that they are a man who studies Spanish.

Alternative acceptable answer:
$\frac{9}{65}$

$\frac{18}{130}$ ✓ ✓

(2)

(Total for Question 17 is 5 marks)

101

18 Simon has £200 and 3700 rand.

He goes to a shop where he can spend both pounds and rand.

He wants to buy:

    a computer costing £360

or

    a watch costing £400

or

    a camera costing £375

The conversion rate is £1 = 21.62 rand.

Which of these items can Simon afford to buy?
You must show clearly how you get your answer.

3700 rand = 3700 ÷ 21.62 = £171.14 ✓

Simon has £200 + £171.14 = £371.14 ✓

Simon can only buy the computer. ✓

(Total for Question 18 is 3 marks)

102

19 A bank pays compound interest of 9.25% per annum.
Ravina invests £8600 for 3 years.

(a) Calculate the interest earned after 3 years.

$8600 \times 1.0925^3 = 11\,214.06$ (2 d.p.) ✓

$11\,214.06 - 8600 = 2614.06$ ✓

£ 2614.06 ✓

(3)

(b) Show that the interest gained after 3 years is 30.4% of her original investment.

$\frac{2614.06}{8600} \times 100\% = 30.4\%$ (1 d.p.) ✓

✓

Alternative acceptable answer:

$1.0925^3 = 1.304$ so percentage increase
         = 30.4%

(2)

(Total for Question 19 is 5 marks)

103

20 Rob is making a scale model of the Solar System on the school field.
He wants the distance from the Sun to Jupiter to be 8 metres on his scale model.

The real distance from the Sun to Jupiter is 7.8×10^8 kilometres.

Find the scale of the model.
Give your answer in the form 1 : n, where n is written in standard form.

$7.8 \times 10^8 \times 1000 = 7.8 \times 10^{11}$ m ✓

$8 : 7.8 \times 10^{11}$

÷8 ↓   ↓ ÷8 ✓

$1 : 9.75 \times 10^{10}$

1 : 9.75 × 10¹⁰ ✓

(Total for Question 20 is 3 marks)

104

159

21 A steel rod has a density of 7.6 g per cm³.
The rod has a mass of 200 g.

Work out the volume of the rod.
Give your answer correct to 3 significant figures.

steel rod

$$V = \frac{M}{D} = \frac{200}{7.6} = 26.31578\ldots \checkmark$$

$\checkmark$ $\checkmark$
26.3 cm³

(Total for Question 21 is 3 marks)

105

22 The diagram shows a side view of a kitchen step ladder.

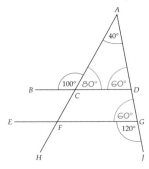

Brian says the straight lines BCD and EFG are parallel.

Is Brian correct?
You must show all your working.
Give reasons for your answer.

Angle $ACD = 180° - 100° = 80°$
(Angles on a straight line add up to 180°)
Angle $CDA = 180° - 40° - 80° = 60°$
(Angles in a triangle add up to 180°) $\checkmark$
Angle $FGD = 180° - 120° = 60°$
(Angles on a straight line add up to 180°) $\checkmark$
So corresponding angles are equal, and BCD and
EFG are parallel. $\checkmark$

(Total for Question 22 is 3 marks)

106

23 PQR is the side of a vertical building.

AB is a ramp.
AP is horizontal ground.
BQ is a horizontal path.

The building has a height of 27 m.
The ramp AB is at an angle of 16° to the horizontal ground.
The ramp has a length of 12 m. The path has a length of 18 m.

(a) Work out the height of the ramp.
Give your answer correct to 3 significant figures.

$$S^O_H\ C^A_H\ T^O_A$$

$$\sin 16° = \frac{h}{12} \checkmark$$

$$h = 12 \times \sin 16° = 3.3076\ldots$$

3.31 $\checkmark$ m

(2)

(b) Show that the angle of elevation of the top of the building, R, from the top of the ramp, B, is 52.8° correct to 3 significant figures.

$$S^O_H\ C^A_H\ T^O_A$$

$$\tan x = \frac{27 - 3.3076\ldots}{18} \checkmark$$
$\checkmark$

$$= 1.3162\ldots$$

$$x = 52.7746\ldots \approx 52.8° \checkmark$$

(3)

(Total for Question 23 is 5 marks)

107

24 Here is a sketch of the curve with equation $y = (x - 2)(x - 8)$

Work out the coordinates of the minimum point, M, of the curve.

Graph crosses x-axis at $x = 2$ and $x = 8$ $\checkmark$
x-coordinate of minimum point $= (2 + 8) \div 2$
$$= 10 \div 2$$
$$= 5$$
When $x = 5$,
$$y = (5 - 2)(5 - 8) = 3 \times -3$$
$\checkmark$ $= -9$

(5 $\checkmark$, -9 $\checkmark$)

(Total for Question 24 is 4 marks)

TOTAL FOR PAPER IS 80 MARKS

108

Paper 3: Calculator
Time allowed: 1 hour 30 minutes

1 Write down 23 507 to the nearest thousand.

24 000 ✓
(Total for Question 1 is 1 mark)

2 (a) Simplify $3m + 7m - 2m$

8m ✓
(1)

(b) Simplify $a^3 + a^3$

$2a^3$ ✓
(1)
(Total for Question 2 is 2 marks)

3 Here are five fractions.

$\frac{5}{20}$ $\frac{9}{36}$ $\frac{25}{100}$ $\frac{12}{52}$ $\frac{17}{68}$

(a) Find which one of these is **not** equal to $\frac{1}{4}$

$\frac{12}{52}$ ✓
(1)

(b) Find a fraction between $\frac{1}{6}$ and $\frac{1}{5}$

$\frac{1}{6} = \frac{10}{60}$ $\frac{1}{5} = \frac{12}{60}$ ✓

Alternative acceptable answers:
Any fraction with a value
between $\frac{1}{6}$ and $\frac{1}{5}$

$\frac{11}{60}$ ✓
(2)
(Total for Question 3 is 3 marks)

4 Here is a list of eight numbers

4   5   25   29   30   33   39   40

From the list, write down

(a) a factor of 20

Alternative acceptable answer:
5

4 ✓

(b) a multiple of 10

Alternative acceptable answer:
40

30 ✓

(c) a prime number that is greater than 15

29 ✓
(Total for Question 4 is 3 marks)

5 A scientist recorded the lengths and the weights of 8 dolphins.
The scatter graph shows information about these dolphins.

(a) Describe the relationship between the length and the weight
of these dolphins.

Positive correlation ✓

Alternative acceptable answer:
As the length increases the weight increases.
(1)

A dolphin has a length of 2.54 metres and a weight of 132 kg.

(b) Show this information on the scatter graph.
(1)

A dolphin has a length of 2.3 metres.

(c) Estimate the weight of this dolphin.

Alternative acceptable answer:
Answers between 118 and 124

121 ✓ kg
(2)

(d) Comment on the reliability of the answer in part (c).

The estimate is reliable because 2.3 m is within the
range of the data (interpolation). ✓
(1)

Alternative acceptable answers:
Estimate is reliable because there is strong
positive correlation.
Estimate is unreliable because it is based on a line
of best fit/scatter graph.
Estimate is unreliable because there aren't very
many data points.

(Total for Question 5 is 5 marks)

6 Solve $2x + 3 = 10$ (-3)

$2x = 7$ $(\div 2)$ ✓

$x = 3.5$

$$x = \underset{\text{3.5 ✓}}{\quad\quad\quad}$$

(Total for Question 6 is 2 marks)

113

---

7 Simon goes to a car boot sale.

He buys:

    4 cups and saucers for a total of £15.95
    4 plates at £1.35 each
    6 egg cups for a total of £7.20.

Simon sells all the items he buys for a total of £45.75.

Does he make a profit or a loss?
You must show all your working.

$4 \times £1.35 = £5.40$ ✓

$£15.95 + £5.40 + £7.20 = £28.55$

✓

$£45.75 > £28.55$ ✓

Simon makes a profit. ✓

(Total for Question 7 is 4 marks)

114

---

8 Expand $3(2 + t)$

3×2

$3(2 + t)$

$3 \times t$

$6 + 3t$ ✓

(Total for Question 8 is 1 mark)

9 Expand $3x(2x + 5)$

$3x \times 2x$

$3x(2x + 5)$

$3x \times 5$

✓ ✓

$6x^2 + 15x$

(Total for Question 9 is 2 marks)

115

---

10 Jeremy invests £300 for two years at 4% simple interest each year.

(a) Work out the amount of interest he will get at the end of two years.

$\dfrac{4}{100} \times 300 = 12$ ✓

$12 \times 2 = 24$

✓

$£\underset{\text{24 ✓}}{\quad\quad\quad}$

(3)

Jeremy buys a TV.
He pays £450 plus 20% VAT.

(b) Work out the VAT.

$\dfrac{20}{100} \times 450 = 90$

✓

$£\underset{\text{90 ✓}}{\quad\quad\quad}$

(2)

(Total for Question 10 is 5 marks)

116

11

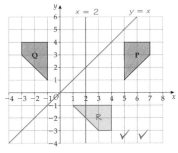

(a) Describe fully the single transformation which maps shape **P** onto shape **Q**.

   ✓

   Reflection in the line $x = 2$ ✓

(2)

(b) Reflect the shape **Q** in the line $y = x$
Label the new shape **R**.

(2)

(Total for Question 11 is 4 marks)

117

12 The map shows the distances, in kilometres, between some towns and cities in France.

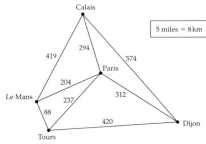

Fiona is on holiday in France.
She drives from Calais to Paris.
She then drives from Paris to Dijon.

Work out the total distance she travels in miles.

294 + 312 = 606 km ✓

$\dfrac{606}{8} \times 5 = 378.75$ miles

   ✓

378.75 ✓ .... miles

(Total for Question 12 is 3 marks)

118

13 (a) Work out $\dfrac{4.6 + 3.85}{3.2^2 - 6.51}$

Write down all the numbers on your calculator display.

4.6 + 3.85 = 8.45

$3.2^2 - 6.51 = 3.73$ ✓

$\dfrac{8.45}{3.73} = 2.26541555$

2.26541555 ✓
(2)

(b) Write down your answer correct to 3 significant figures.

2.27 ✓
(1)

(Total for Question 13 is 3 marks)

119

14 The diagram shows the positions of two villages, Beckhampton (*B*) and West Kennett (*W*). The diagram is drawn accurately.

Scale: 4 cm represents 1 km.

(a) Work out the real distance, in kilometres, of Beckhampton from West Kennett.

10 cm

10 ÷ 4 = 2.5

   ✓

2.5 ✓ .... km
(2)

The village Avebury (*A*) is on a bearing of 038° from Beckhampton.

On the diagram, *A* is 6 cm from *B*.

(b) On the diagram, mark *A* with a cross (×).
Label the cross *A*.

(2)

(Total for Question 14 is 4 marks)

120

163

15 The speed, v, of a car is 73 miles per hour, correct to the nearest whole number.

Write down the error interval for the speed of the car.

Accuracy is to nearest 1 mile so
lower bound = 73 − 0.5
upper bound = 73 + 0.5

72.5 ✓ ≤ v < 73.5 ✓

(Total for Question 15 is 2 marks)

121

122

16 Here is an accurate scale diagram of a car park in the shape of a rectangle.

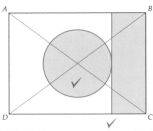

The scale is 1 cm to 10 m.

Cars must **not** be parked:

within 20 m of the centre of the rectangle

or

within 20 m of the side BC.

On the diagram, show accurately by shading, the regions where cars must not be parked.

(Total for Question 16 is 4 marks)

17 Factorise $x^2 + 7x$

$x(x + 7)$ ✓

(Total for Question 17 is 1 mark)

18 Factorise $y^2 - 10y + 16$

$(-8) + (-2) = -10$
$(-8) \times (-2) = 16$

$(y - 8)(y - 2)$ ✓ ✓

(Total for Question 18 is 2 marks)

123

124

19 The distance of the Earth from Mars is 5.5×10^7 kilometres.

(a) Write 5.5×10^7 as an ordinary number.

55 000 000 ✓
(1)

The diameter of Jupiter is 143 000 kilometres.

(b) Write 143 000 in standard form.

1.43×10^5 ✓
(1)

One light year is the distance travelled by light in one year.

One astronomical unit (au) is the average distance from the Sun to the Earth.

One light year = 9.461×10^{12} km
One astronomical unit = 1.496×10^8 km

(c) How many astronomical units are there in a light year?

Give your answer in standard form correct to 3 significant figures.

$9.461 \times 10^{12} \div 1.496 \times 10^8 = 63\,241.978\,61$ ✓

6.32×10^4 ✓ au
(2)

(Total for Question 19 is 4 marks)

20 Greg sells car insurance and home insurance.
The table shows the cost of these insurances.

Insurance	Car insurance	Home insurance
Cost	£200	£350

Each month Greg earns:
    £530 basic pay plus
    5% commission of the cost of all the car insurance he sells
and   10% commission of the cost of all the home insurance he sells.

In May, Greg sold:
    6 car insurances
and   4 home insurances.

Work out the total amount of money Greg earned in May.

$\frac{5}{100} \times 200 = 10$ ✓

$\frac{10}{100} \times 350 = 35$

✓   ✓
$530 + 6 \times 10 + 4 \times 35 = 530 + 60 + 140$
$= 730$

£ ......730...... ✓

(Total for Question 20 is 4 marks)

125

21 In a sale the price of paving slabs is reduced by 70%.
Josie buys some paving slabs at the sale price of £90.

What was the original price of the paving slabs?

$100\% - 70\% = 30\%$ ✓

$\frac{30\%}{100\%} = 0.3$

$90 \div 0.3 = 300$

£ ......300...... ✓

(2)
(Total for Question 21 is 2 marks)

126

22 Use a ruler and compasses to construct the bisector of this angle.
You must show all your construction lines.

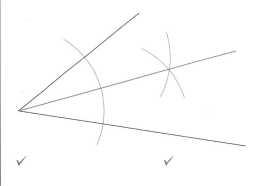

✓   ✓

(Total for Question 22 is 2 marks)

127

23 A box contains some coloured cards.
Each card is red or blue or yellow or green.
The table shows the probability of taking a red card or a blue card or a yellow card.

Card	Probability
Red	0.3
Blue	0.35
Yellow	0.15
Green	

George takes, at random, a card from the box.

(a) Work out the probability that George takes a green card.

$0.3 + 0.35 + 0.15 = 0.8$
$1 - 0.8 = 0.2$
✓

......0.2...... ✓
(2)

George replaces his card in the box.
Anish takes a card from the box and then replaces the card.
Anish does this 40 times.

(b) Work out an estimate for the number of times Anish takes a yellow card.

$0.15 \times 40 = 6$
✓

......6...... ✓
(2)
(Total for Question 23 is 4 marks)

128

165

24 The diagram shows a right-angled triangle and a rectangle.

9 cm

7 cm

(8x + 4) cm

(10 − x) cm

The area of the triangle is twice the area of the rectangle.

Find the area of the rectangle.
Show clear algebraic working.

Area of triangle $= \frac{1}{2} \times$ base $\times$ height
$= \frac{1}{2}(8x + 4) \times 9$
$= (4x + 2) \times 9$
$= 36x + 18$ ✓

Area of rectangle $=$ length $\times$ width
$= (10 − x) \times 7$
$= 70 − 7x$

$36x + 18 = 2(70 − 7x)$ ✓
$36x + 18 = 140 − 14x$ (+ 14x)
$50x + 18 = 140$ (− 18)
$50x = 122$
$x = 2.44$ ✓

Area of rectangle $= (10 − 2.44) \times 7$
$= 7.56 \times 7 = 52.92 \text{ cm}^2$ ✓

<u>52.92</u> ✓ cm²

(Total for Question 24 is 5 marks)

129

25 The table shows information about the amount of money, in dollars, spent in a shop in one day by 80 people.

Money spent (x dollars)	Frequency	Midpoint, x	f × x
$0 < x \le 20$	24	10	24 × 10 = 240
$20 < x \le 40$	20	30	20 × 30 = 600
$40 < x \le 60$	9	50	9 × 50 = 450
$60 < x \le 80$	12	70	12 × 70 = 840
$80 < x \le 100$	15	90	15 × 90 = 1350
Totals	80		3480

(a) Write down the modal class interval.

$0 < x \le 20$ ✓

(1)

(b) Work out an estimate for the mean amount of money spent in that shop that day.

$\dfrac{3480}{80}$ ✓ $= 43.5$ ✓

43.50 ✓ dollars

(3)

One more person spent 84 dollars.

(c) How will this affect the mean?

You must give a reason.

84 is greater than 43.5 so the mean will increase. ✓

(1)

(Total for Question 25 is 5 marks)

130

26 The diagram shows a parallelogram, PQRS.

M is the midpoint of PS.
$\overrightarrow{PM} = \mathbf{a}$ $\overrightarrow{PQ} = \mathbf{b}$

Find, in terms of **a** and/or **b**:

(a) $\overrightarrow{PS}$

$\overrightarrow{PS} = 2 \times \overrightarrow{PM}$

2a ✓

(1)

(b) $\overrightarrow{PR}$

$\overrightarrow{PR} = \overrightarrow{PS} + \overrightarrow{SR}$

2a + b ✓

(1)

(c) $\overrightarrow{MQ}$

$\overrightarrow{MQ} = \overrightarrow{MP} + \overrightarrow{PQ}$

−a + b ✓

(1)

(Total for Question 26 is 3 marks)

TOTAL FOR PAPER IS 80 MARKS

131

166

Notes

Notes

Notes

Notes

Notes

Notes